Changing offenders' attitudes and behaviour: what works?

Part I:
The use of cognitive-behavioural approaches with offenders: messages from the research.

Julie Vennard, Darren Sugg and Carol Hedderman

Part II:
The influence of cognitive approaches: a survey of probation programmes.

Carol Hedderman and Darren Sugg

A Research and Statistics Directorate Report

Home Office
Research and
Statistics
Directorate

London: Home Office

Home Office Research Studies

The Home Office Research Studies are reports on research undertaken by or on behalf of the Home Office. They cover the range of subjects for which the Home Secretary has responsibility. Titles in the series are listed at the back of this report (copies are available from the address on the back cover). Other publications produced by the Research and Statistics Directorate include Research Findings, the Research Bulletin, Statistical Bulletins and Statistical Papers.

The Research and Statistics Directorate

The Directorate consists of three Units which deal with research and statistics on Crime and Criminal Justice, Offenders and Corrections, Immigration and General Matters; the Programme Development Unit; the Economics Unit; and the Operational Research Unit.

The Research and Statistics Directorate is an integral part of the Home Office, serving the Ministers and the department itself, its services, Parliament and the public through research, development and statistics. Information and knowledge from these sources informs policy development and the management of programmes; their dissemination improves wider public understanding of matters of Home Office concern.

First published 1997

Application for reproduction should be made to the Information and Publications Group, Room 201, Home Office, 50 Queen Anne's Gate, London SW1H 9AT.

©Crown copyright 1997 ISBN 1 85893 904 6
ISSN 0072 6435

Foreword

Offender programmes which draw on the psychological theories and techniques of cognitive-behaviourism seek to modify patterns of thinking and reduce offending behaviour. This research was undertaken with a view to increasing understanding of the effectiveness of cognitive-behavioural interventions with offenders and providing information about their use by probation services in England and Wales.

The first part of the report reviews the findings of relevant research studies. It considers the range of techniques subsumed within the cognitive–behavioural framework, the methods used to gauge their effectiveness and the conclusion which can be safely drawn about their impact on offending behaviour.

The second part of the report describes the results of a national survey of probation service programmes which draw on cognitive-behavioural methods. What types of offender are selected for these programmes, how are the programmes managed and resourced and to what extent do probation services measure their impact on offenders' attitudes and ways of behaving?

Together the literature review and the survey provide a valuable source of information for policy makers, researchers and those involved in managing or delivering offender programmes. They also sugggest ways in which probation services can strengthen programmes which draw on cognitive-behavioural approaches and improve their understanding of the components and techniques which work best with different types of offender.

CHRIS LEWIS
Head of Offenders and Corrections Unit
Research and Statistics Directorate
July 1997

Acknowledgements

The authors would like to thank all of the Chief Officers of Probation who agreed to their services taking part in the survey and the individual respondents tasked with providing the information we required. We are also grateful to James McGuire for valuable comments on an early draft of the literature review.

Carol Hedderman
Darren Sugg
Julie Vennard

Contents

Summary

The use of cognitive–behavioural approaches with offenders: messages from the research

Over the last decade, research has suggested that some forms of rehabilitative work can be effective in reducing reoffending. Among the range of methods of working with offenders, those encompassed within the term 'cognitive-behavioural' are increasingly favoured. They are widely viewed as offering considerable advantages over more traditional forms of intervention. Because this term is so broad it is difficult to define precisely, but it involves helping offenders to face up to the consequences of their actions, to understand their motives, and to develop new ways of controlling their behaviour.

This review examines the evidence on the application and effectiveness of cognitive-behavioural approaches with offenders. It also draws lessons from the literature about the successful delivery and management of such programmes.

The main points to emerge from the review are:

- The effectiveness of interventions with offenders varies significantly according to the type of approach adopted. Programmes which seek to modify offenders' patterns of thinking and behaving are generally more successful than techniques such as group or individual counselling and non-directive therapy.

- Even these approaches rarely produce major reductions in reoffending among offenders in general. This supports the view that programme components and styles of delivery need to be closely matched to the needs and learning styles of particular offenders.

- The use of cognitive-behavioural methods in programmes which also include training in social skills (for example, teaching sex offenders to form appropriate relationships with other adults) show the most positive results with both juvenile and adult offenders.

- Lack of agreement about how to classify the range of techniques encompassed by the cognitive-behavioural approach means that it is not possible to identify precisely which particular forms of intervention are most promising.

- The research shows that the impact of cognitive-behavioural methods of working with offenders can be enhanced by:

    - targetting on factors which have contributed to the offending behaviour

    - using active, participatory, problem solving methods of working

    - matching the intensity and duration of intervention to likely future risk of offending

    - running programmes as intended, without allowing the goals and methods to shift over time.

Implications for policy, practice and future research

The positive, but inconclusive, findings of the reviews summarised in the report raise a number of issues for those involved in the delivery and management of offender programmes.

- Researchers and practitioners working with offenders need to develop and agree definitions for the various components of cognitive-behavioural methods. More also needs to be known about what type of approach works best, under what conditions and types of setting, with whom.

- Offenders should be assessed and allocated to programmes according to their particular needs and learning styles. Although cognitive-behavioural methods can yield the most successful outcomes, they are unlikely to work unless other principles concerning effective programmes are followed.

- Effective use of cognitive-behavioural approaches requires a fuller knowledge of the underlying principles, theories and techniques than most probation officers currently possess.

- Those undertaking and managing work with offenders need to become more responsive to the need to evaluate their work. Programmes included in an evaluation need to make explicit the underlying theory as to how they expect to effect change, the content and method of intervention, and the framework for implementation.

The influence of cognitive approaches: a survey of probation programmes

In February 1996 the Offenders and Corrections Unit of the Home Office sent out a questionnaire to all probation areas asking for information about the extent to which the programmes they operated, or had access to, made use of cognitive skills training. Cognitive skills was defined for the purposes of this survey as an approach which attempted to reduce reoffending by teaching offenders to analyse and modify their thinking.

The results of the survey are:

- Forty-three areas replied–a response rate of 78 per cent. Of these four did not run programmes with a cognitive skills component. The remaining 39 areas ran 191 such programmes. Only half of these had been running for more than five years; and a quarter had been running for less than a year.

- The decision to set up cognitive behavioural programmes was often influenced by a combination of factors: 53 per cent of respondents cited successful results in other probation areas; 44 per cent said the approach had been championed by a member of staff; and a third of programmes–mainly those dealing with sex offenders or self control programmes–had been influenced by research from abroad.

- Only 35 programmes in 17 areas were bought-in as opposed to being developed locally. The fact that the intensity and duration of these (highly structured) programmes were so often altered suggests that insufficient attention was being given to ensuring that programmes were delivered as intended.

- General programmes were more popular than those which focused on a particular form of offending. Among the latter, those for treating sex offenders and for tackling poor driving behaviour were the most common.

- Programmes seemed to function without reference to risk and needs principles. While most were primarily run for those attending as a condition of a court order, few excluded participation by other offenders attending on a voluntary basis. Mixing offenders in this way may be an efficient use of resources, but is unlikely to achieve programmes which are well matched to levels of risk, and offending-related needs.

- Sex offender programmes tend to be (comparatively) well-organised, run by well-trained staff, and able to draw on outside expertise, but they too are rarely restricted to serious offenders.

- Programmes should either be staffed by appropriately trained probation officers; or involve specialists through partnership arrangements. Yet 24 per cent of probation staff had received no extra training at all and 105 programmes were run without any other agencies being involved.

- The limited information provided on costs shows that specialist such programmes do not come cheap, yet areas have spent surprisingly little time or effort on examining whether such programmes work. In most areas it seems that they do not even know how many people attend, who drops out and why, and who succeeds and why.

Perhaps the most encouraging aspect of our findings was that respondents were far from complacent about the way programmes were operating. Many of those responsible for running the programmes on a day-to-day basis would clearly welcome more training, more advice and better evaluations. One obvious improvement would be for a more strategic approach to setting up and running programmes at senior levels, with programmes being piloted and evaluated before being delivered on a larger scale. Another might be to create a standard set of evaluation measures which would ensure that similar programmes were being compared fairly.

Part I:
The use of cognitive-behavioural approaches with offenders: messages from the research.

Julie Vennard, Darren Sugg and Carol Hedderman

The use of cognitive-behavioural approaches with offenders: messages from the research

Introduction

Community and prison based programmes designed to rehabilitate offenders have been criticised over recent decades on two main grounds. First, that they over simplify the roots of offending behaviour and take too little account of adverse social and economic circumstances. Second, that there is a lack of research evidence demonstrating the effectiveness of such interventions. This so called 'nothing works' position has given way in recent years to a cautious optimism, supported by a growing body of research evidence, that some types of intervention can be effective in reducing offending.

Among the range of offender programmes designed to reintegrate offenders into society, those which are increasingly favoured, both in institutional and community settings, seek to address deficiencies in offenders' ways of thinking, reasoning and associated behaviour through what are termed 'cognitive-behavioural' techniques. The main aim of this review is to summarise the available research findings on the effectiveness of such interventions in reducing offending and achieving beneficial attitude or behavioural changes. This introductory section describes the context and scope of the review. The next considers what is commonly understood by the term cognitive behaviourism in the context of rehabilitative programmes undertaken with offenders. The third section summarises the ways in which researchers have approached the broad question 'what works', since it is within this body of research that any evidence of the impact of cognitive-behavioural techniques is to be found. Consideration is then given to the findings of the research, followed by a brief discussion of some possible implications of the findings for the design and delivery of effective programmes with offenders. The concluding section summarises the broad messages and the gaps in the research literature with regard to the effectiveness of cognitive-behavioural interventions and identifies areas in which further research is needed.

During the 1970s and 1980s scepticism regarding the efficacy of individualised 'treatment' of offenders, which attributes criminal conduct to the particular personality and circumstances of the individual, was heavily influenced by a study undertaken in the United States by Martinson (1974). Under pressure to demonstrate that time spent in prison can achieve rehabilitative as well as punitive aims, in 1966 the prison service in New York State commissioned Robert Martinson to undertake a review of the available research. The central message to emerge from the review, which was based upon 231 studies of rehabilitative programmes carried out in a variety of institutional and non-institutional settings published in the English language over a 22 - year period, was that, with few and isolated exceptions, the treatment studied had no significant impact on further offending.

In seeking to explain his findings Martinson postulated that there may be a "radical flaw in our present strategies–that education at its best or that psychotherapy at its best cannot overcome, or even appreciably reduce, the powerful tendency for offenders to continue in their criminal behaviour". Martinson entered a number of caveats about his findings, including the poor quality of many of the original studies, lack of comparability in the measurement of reoffending and the heterogeneity of the groups studied. It is also noteworthy that in his original article Martinson acknowledged the possibility that some treatment programmes *are* working to some extent, but that methodological weaknesses in the original studies prevent any pattern being detected. These caveats tended, however, to be overlooked by those who saw in the article strong empirical support for the rejection of a treatment approach and for return to a 'just deserts' perspective, in which the principle of appropriate and proportionate punishment is paramount in the sentencing decision.

Perhaps unsurprisingly, many practitioners and specialists working with offenders during this period continued to believe that appropriately targetted interventions could bring about a reduction in offending. McGuire and Priestley (1995) observe that, from the outset a number of researchers (notably Gendreau and Ross, 1979) expressed reservations about the 'nothing works' doctrine and were able to find some evidence of positive outcomes from better controlled studies, often the same types of intervention as those evaluated by Martinson. Gendreau (1995) has commented more recently that, despite the disaffection with rehabilitation in the US, in Canada the rehabilitative agenda continued to flourish through the 1970s and 1980s, academics and government officials continuing to promote and research rehabilitative programmes.

The resurgence of confidence in Britain in the rehabilitative potential of probation can be attributed in large part to the findings from Canadian and North American research. Recent years have also witnessed an increasing number of conferences in this country, attended by policy-makers, researchers and practitioners, on the subject of research and practice concerning effective interventions with offenders. At one such conference, sponsored by the Home Office, Association of Chief Officers of Probation and the Central Probation Council, delegates met to consider how the results of this emerging research might best be put into practice through improved management of community supervision programmes.

Following this 'Managing What Works' conference, Probation Circular

77/1995 required Chief Probation Officers to review their current and planned programmes against a list of 'critical success factors' adapted from research and from the conference proceedings. These principles have been widely endorsed by a number of researchers who have reviewed some of the better designed studies of rehabilitative programmes (e.g. Andrews et al., 1990; Hollin, 1994; Lipsey, 1992; McGuire, 1995) and are now familiar to probation officers in this country. They are described in the literature in the following terms:

- *Risk classification*-more intensive programmes should be targetted at high risk offenders, while those of lower risk should receive lower or minimal intervention;

- *Targeting criminogenic needs*-it is important to differentiate between 'criminogenic needs' (those factors which contribute directly to criminal behaviour, such as anti-social attitudes, drug dependency, limited cognitive skills) and needs which have no direct relationship with propensity to reoffend. If the purpose of the programme is to reduce offending the focus should be upon criminogenic needs

- *Responsivity*-match the learning styles of the offenders to the teaching styles of those providing the programmes. The learning styles of most offenders require active, participatory approaches rather than traditional client-centred counselling

- *Treatment modality*-linked with responsiveness, this principle states that appropriate types of intervention are typically skills oriented (designed to improve problem-solving, social interaction and other types of 'coping' skills) and draw upon cognitive-behavioural and social learning methods

- *Community base*-generally community-based programmes have shown more positive results, but programmes which take into account risk, criminogenic need and responsiveness can work in any treatment setting

- *Programme integrity*-programmes should be properly managed andcarried out by trained staff in accordance with clearly identified aims and objectives that do not change over time.

In promoting these principles throughout the probation service in the form of a Home Office circular, it is hoped that they will be translated into effective local practice when assessing risk and need and allocating offenders to suitable programmes. The Prison Service is similarly seeking to improve the effectiveness of its offender programmes, having regard to the available research evidence. Drawing on the findings reported by Hollin and Palmer (1995) in a literature review commissioned by the Prison Service, prison based programmes must now meet a number of accreditation criteria, one of which is that they should combine both cognitive and behavioural techniques drawn from social learning theory.

The adoption of cognitive-behavioural approaches has been much in evidence in a range of institutional and community settings in Canada and their efficacy has been examined in the wider context of seeking to develop knowledge about the ingredients of successful interventions with offenders. Cognitive-behavioural approaches have also been used in the probation service in England and Wales for some time, notably the Reasoning and Rehabilitation programme developed in Canada by Ross, Fabiano and Ross, (1989); and there is evidence from a recent study by Burnett (1996) that close to a third of probation officers favour a cognitive-behavioural approach in their work with offenders. Our own survey of the use of these techniques by the probation service indicates that by mid 1996 at least 39 of the 54 probation areas in England and Wales were running programmes which employed cognitive skills or cognitive-behavioural techniques. It is important to be clear, therefore, about the advantages to be gained from the use of this mode of treatment with offenders.

In a recent critique of meta-analysis and of its role in the 'nothing works' debate, Mair and Copas (1996) contend that the existing meta-analytic reviews cannot, in fact, offer principles for successful interventions with any confidence, since information is lacking on precisely *what* works, *how* it achieves its impact and in *what* conditions. The need for a fuller understanding of the ingredients of effective intervention, as applied to specific offender groups, is, in fact, recognised by leading meta-analysts. Gendreau and Andrews, (1990), for example, acknowledge the limitations of the technique and identify a number of unanswered questions concerning the components and contexts of effective treatment programmes. Other writers (e.g., Lab and Whitehead, 1990) have observed there needs to be an explicit understanding as to the criteria practitioners should apply when judging risk, need and appropriate types of intervention if the broad success factors are to be consistently applied to practice.

With these caveats in mind, what can be drawn from the research evidence with regard to the application and effectiveness of cognitive-behavioural forms of intervention with offenders? Specific questions which this paper seeks to answer are :

- what types of approach are encompassed within the term cognitive-behavioural

- how has the impact of this approach, and others used in interventions with offenders been evaluated

- what evidence exists of the benefits of cognitive-behavioural approaches in reducing further offending

- what is the available evidence on the types of approach which are most effective with different groups of offenders

- what lessons can be drawn from the literature regarding the requirements for successful delivery and management of cognitive-behavioural programmes.

It should be said at the outset that it is not an intention of this paper to provide a detailed review of the full range of individual studies (most of which are Canadian or North American) which have examined the impact of cognitive-behavioural programmes. Most of the published studies have already been examined and generally, the more robust ones have been synthesised in traditional or meta-analytic literature reviews reported over the past decade. This paper draws primarily on the most extensive and more recent of these reviews in seeking to answer the above questions.

Cognitive-behaviourism: theory and techniques

Cognitive behaviourism is not a unified, distinct psychological theory or method but a term given to a range of interventions derived from the following three psychological theories:

- *behaviourism*, which stresses the role of external, environmental factors in shaping an individual's actions so that, for offenders, for example, encouragement from peers and/or the lack of immediate punishment from authority figures reinforces criminal behaviour (Blackburn, 1995)

- *cognitive theory*, in which the importance of an individual's thought processes, such as reasoning, memory and problem solving are stressed. As Hollin notes, *"cognition is implicit in the theories of writers who suggest that various styles of thinking, such as 'impulsive and concrete', are characteristic of offender populations"*(Ausubel, 1958; Glueck and Glueck, 1950; Hollin, 1990, p 10)

- *social learning theory*, which is derived from behaviourism but states that, while the environment remains a key factor, learning may also occur indirectly, through observation of outcomes of the behaviour of others. The impact of the environment on behaviour is thus mediated by cognition (Hollin, 1990).

In a course manual on cognitive-behavioural theory and research McGuire (1996) describes the way in which the ideas from behavioural and cognitive traditions within psychology and psychotherapy were integrated, in the 1970s, into a new approach to understanding the "complex dynamic relationships between thoughts, feelings and behaviour". As an approach to working with offenders, cognitive-behavioural modification assumes that offenders are shaped by their environment and have failed to acquire certain cognitive skills or have learnt inappropriate ways of behaving. Thinking may be impulsive and egocentric, concrete rather than abstract and rigid rather then flexible. McGuire stresses, however, that a cognitive-behavioural approach does not attribute the causes of criminal behaviour solely to individual or psychological factors. It also takes into account the social conditions which affect individual development and is not in conflict with sociological explanations of criminal activity, such as those which view such behaviour as acquired from influential delinquent peer groups.

Since it is considered that such cognitive deficits are learned rather than inherent, offender programmes based on this conceptualisation of human behaviour are intended to teach offenders to face up to what they have done, to understand their motives and to develop new coping strategies and ways of controlling their behaviour. This can be accomplished using a range of behavioural and cognitive techniques. *Behavioural modification* typically seek to reinforce socially acceptable behaviours through techniques such as contingency contracts, according to which offenders agree to behave in certain ways and are rewarded for doing so. Rewards for achieving specific targets may take the form of approval, desired activities or token reinforcers which provide access to such activities. Self-reinforcement techniques may also be used, whereby offenders monitor and evaluate their own behaviour (Hollin, 1993). *Behaviour therapy* is also based upon the theory of conditioned learning but focuses on reducing unwanted patterns of thought and behaviour through such techniques as relaxation training (reduction in levels of arousal), training and assertiveness training designed to replace anxiety and similar emotions with positive coping responses (McGuire, 1996). The distinctive characteristic of *cognitive therapy*, which McGuire describes as the most 'cognitively oriented' form of cognitive-behavioural therapy, is that it seeks to identify and modify dysfunctional, distorted thoughts, replacing them with more adaptive thinking patterns.

Cognitive-behavioural interventions which seek to improve self control draw on behavioural techniques such as self-monitoring, self-reinforcement and *self-instructional training* (SET), in which covert 'inner' speech is used to control overt behaviour. McGuire (1996) describes self-instructional training as a standard feature of the cognitive-behavioural approach, though he notes that it is widely used in combination with other types of method. As an approach to self regulation, SET may, in fact, be viewed as more closely linked to cognitive learning than to behavioural conditioning and illustrates the difficulty in categorising the range of techniques encompassed by the cognitive-behavioural label.

Also subsumed within the cognitive-behavioural framework are certain other related and overlapping approaches. *Social skills training,* a form of behavioural therapy, is sometimes used in conjunction with cognitive techniques as a method of increasing skills for dealing with social encounters. This technique is commonly employed with young offenders and sex offenders whose offending is thought to derive, at least in part, from their lack of self-esteem and inability to deal with other adults appropriately or effectively. The objective may be to develop 'micro' skills such as eye contact and body posture, or 'macro' skills such as communication with parents and resisting pressure from delinquent peers. The methods adopted in social skills programmes include instruction concerning standards of behaviour and expectations, modelling (presentation of a coping response in a given social situation), role play, rehearsal, feedback and social reinforcement. Observing that some category boundaries are still somewhat fluid, Palmer (1994) notes that social skills training is classified variously as "cognitive skills", "cognitive-behavioural", "social cognitive" or "skills oriented", the latter sometimes being used as a generic term to encompass 'life skills' (a wide range of practical skills such a literacy and numeracy) as well as 'social skills'. Skills training programmes may be blended with *problem-solving training,* which seeks to improve problem awareness, perspective taking and the ability to foresee the likely consequences of one's actions. Here again, the skills training techniques of instruction, modelling, discussion and feedback are employed.

As Hollin (1996) and others have observed, programmes for young offenders frequently incorporate a variety of methods, including cognitive-behavioural approaches, into a *multimodal* programme. Key elements are, typically problem solving training, social skills training, anger control and moral education. Although multimodal programmes are increasingly regarded as offering the best chances of successful reduction in reoffending, since they are able to address a wide range of problems and needs, difficulties arise when seeking to identify which components are and are not effective in any given combination. As will be seen, this uncertainty has created fundamental difficulties for those seeking to discriminate between various approaches and to determine what works best with different types of offenders.

How cognitive-behavioural approaches have been evaluated

At around the same time that Martinson (1974) was claiming, albeit with certain qualifications, that nothing worked, other reviewers such as Palmer (1975) and Gendreau and Ross (1979) were asserting that some programmes, including many of those reviewed by Martinson, were, in fact, very successful in addressing offending behaviour. The poor quality of the research methods used in the original studies was regarded as a principal reason for the failure to distinguish such programmes from those which were less successful. The research studies also paid little attention to the processes by which programmes were implemented, so that it was often unclear whether those involved in their delivery adhered to the agreed aims and procedures. Hence, the observation by Mair that:

> "if a large number of the projects Martinson considered were poorly planned, badly implemented, starved of resources, or were administered by untrained and uncommitted staff with a high turnover rate–would it be any surprise to find the programmes had failed?" (Mair, 1995, p 459).

It must also be acknowledged that, as a measure of the success or failure of rehabilitative interventions, reconviction rates are by no means unproblematic. The limitations of reconviction rates have been fully documented elsewhere (e.g. Lloyd, Mair and Hough, 1994) and need to be born in mind when drawing on conclusions from the research literature about the effectiveness of programmes. One difficulty is that in North America, where most of the studies on cognitive-behavioural approaches have been undertaken, the term recidivism is defined in a wide variety of ways and may or may not equate with reconviction in a court for a further offence. Examples of alternative definitions are: arrest for a further offence; parole violation; and violation of a probation order. This obviously creates difficulties for those seeking to compare programmes or to combine the findings from several different experimental studies. A second problem when relying on reconviction rates as an indicator of effectiveness is that, however defined, they almost certainly under-estimate the true level of reoffending. As is well known, approximately half of offences in this country are not reported to the police (Mayhew, Aye Maung and Mirrlees-Black, 1993) and for many types of offence the clear up rate is very low. A further limitation of reconviction rates is lack of clarity concerning the 'correct' follow-up period and when to start counting. Counting begins for those in custody from the date of release, whereas for community penalties it conventionally begins on the date of sentence. There is, however, an argument that the effectiveness of supervision (including any period on parole) should be assessed only when the treatment has been completed.

Other difficulties include the failure of reconviction studies to measure changes in the severity of offending and intervals between offences; and the impact that police and prosecution practices have on whether further offences result in criminal proceedings.

Having themselves carried out one of the largest and most sophisticated British reconviction studies, Lloyd, Mair and Hough caution against uncritical reliance on them as a measure of effectiveness and suggest that in studying the impact of different sentences or programmes the scope for devising additional measures should always be considered. For example, in the case of sex offender treatment programmes offenders can be scored on a range of psychometric tests before and after therapy designed to measure changes in attitudes believed to contribute towards reoffending (see, for example Beckett et al., 1994). It is generally accepted, however, that evaluation studies must seek to demonstrate that any such changes hold up over time and do, in fact, translate into reduced offending rates. Hence, the evaluation of sex offender treatment programmes undertaken by Beckett et al., allowed for the calculation of reconviction rates two years after completion of the programme (Hedderman and Sugg, 1996).

There is some evidence to suggest that the methodological rigour of studies of work with offender groups has improved in recent years. Some large scale programmes, such as the Sex Offender Treatment Evaluation Programme (SOTEP) in California, have used randomised controls, extensive follow up periods and complex statistical procedures (Marques, 1994). Furthermore, evaluations are beginning to study how programmes are delivered (as opposed to how they were designed to operate), and what consequences this has for the outcome as, for example, in a study by Mair et al., (1994) of intensive probation in England and Wales. It is also increasingly the case that evaluation studies include other outcome measures, such as educational achievement, attitude or behavioural change. Few individual studies have, however, provided a sufficiently clear understanding of the causal links between intermediate outcome measures and reconviction to enable replication of the conditions in which successful outcomes have been observed. It was with a view to synthesising the findings from better designed studies, thereby increasing understanding of the ingredients of successful interventions with offenders, that a number of researchers turned to the technique of meta-analysis.

Put simply, this technique involves reducing the characteristics of individual studies into a number of summary statistics, such as number of offenders, the type of treatment given, and recidivism rates (however measured) after treatment. The summary statistics are then analysed to produce an overall "effect size" statistic which represents the *amount* of difference in recidivism that exists between the intervention programme and the respective control programme. One of the main advantages claimed for this technique is that the results from small scale studies, which may be of limited use when considered in isolation, become influential when combined with the results of similar programmes.

There are, however, a number of problems associated with meta-analysis and with the way in which it has been used to aggregate the findings of programmes in the offender corrections field. Without examining these problems in detail it is important to be aware of the limitations of meta-analysis as a method of determining what types of intervention are effective in reducing reoffending.

In their critique of meta-analysis Mair and Copas (1996) distinguish between the use of this technique in order to review research literature systematically –for example, to see if certain programme characteristics are associated with higher effect sizes–and using it to draw broader inferences from the combined results about the relative effectiveness of rehabilitative programmes. They conclude that the former, a purely descriptive technique, is relatively uncontroversial and useful. The latter, which they term Level 11 analysis, is more problematic for several reasons. The main difficulty arises from the use of formal statistical procedures to calculate mean effect sizes for subsets of the studies, grouping, for example, according to design characteristics or type of programme. Since effect sizes are artificial constructs they may fail to take account of important differences in the design of the studies and the offenders sampled. Sample subjects are not, as in controlled trials, selected randomly from a clearly defined population. Rather, the collection of primary studies comprises the sample and it is assumed that the totality of offenders across the studies is representative. Similarly, Level 11 analysis assumes that the interventions are broadly comparable and are delivered in equivalent conditions. Since both types of assumption are unsafe, according to Mair and Copas it follows that meta-analysis cannot predict what would happen if a particular intervention were to be transferred elsewhere or delivered more widely. Others (such as Farrington, 1996) have observed that the way in which meta-analysis has been used to aggregate the results of programmes with offenders glosses over the disparate nature of much of this work, over the different research designs employed in the original studies, and over the various success criteria used.

In fact, the more recent large-scale meta-analyses, such as that carried out by Lipsey (1992), have included an examination of the relationship between the study design, sample size and characteristics, and the effect size distribution. This enabled Lipsey to conclude that effect size does depend substantially upon the methodological characteristics of the study, but it is also importantly influenced by the nature and circumstances of the treatment under study. Lipsey and others concede, however, that treatment modality and the organisational structures and settings in which programmes are delivered, are often described rather poorly in the original studies and are correspondingly difficult to code in a meta-analysis. Consequently, the results are unlikely to be capable of replication elsewhere.

Other difficulties associated with meta-analysis arise from shortcomings in the original programme evaluations and although some researchers have been highly selective (for example, only 46 of the 317 programmes Izzo and Ross (1990) identified met their evaluation criteria) others may have been less rigorous in their selection process. These difficulties exist even when meta-analysis is used simply to describe differences and similarities between studies in order to see what kinds of treatment have been tested with what results.

A particular problem in evaluating cognitive-behavioural programmes arises from the absence of consensus over what this approach encompasses, and whether the types of intervention undertaken in the original studies can legitimately be entitled cognitive-behavioural (Palmer, 1994). Programmes which adopt this approach are often combined with other components and have tended to be defined somewhat differently by meta-analysts. As Palmer observes, this gives rise to problems of interpretation. For example, Panizzon et al., (1991) found little evidence of success with what they termed 'social cognitive interventions' but impressive results for 'role playing/modelling', which others (e.g. Izzo and Ross, 1990) have classified as a form of social cognitive intervention.

When evaluating the results of individual studies meta-analysts and reviewers generally consider that differences between experimental and control groups which achieve the probability level $p<.05$ (i.e. a less than five per cent probability of the result occurring by chance) or its equivalent is an acceptable indicator of the success "or at least promise" (Palmer, 1994). Palmer notes, however, that a few analysts/reviewers employ different criteria and this difference contributes to inconsistent interpretation of the findings. This is illustrated later in relation to the meta-analysis undertaken by Whitehead and Lab (1989) who adopted a stricter criterion of success than is the norm.

There is broad agreement in the research literature that high-risk offenders require more intensive services and conversely, that low risk offenders should receive less intensive intervention. As Palmer (1994) notes, however, the situation with regard to risk is quite complex and although there is some evidence that intensive programmes are most effective with high-risk offenders, "middle risk" offenders have sometimes been more amenable to change. The validity of the risk principle with the highest risk cases remains uncertain because of the paucity of studies of interventions which are both intensive and suitably targetted on offence-related behaviour. Furthermore, inadequate matching between the experimental and the control group on factors pertaining to risk of reoffending will obviously reduce the chances of accurately assessing the impact of a programme. This is thought to have occurred in some of the studies included in meta-analyses, although once again the primary studies have, in fact, tended to say little about methods of selection or suitable participants.

Meta-analyses may also overlook the possibility that work undertaken with comparison groups has been reasonably effective, thus reducing the ability of the research to gauge the impact of the experimental intervention. Indeed, as Palmer (1994) points out, standard programmes run by competent staff, may make a considerable contribution to the goal of reducing reoffending and will thus reduce the difference in the recidivism rates between the experimental and the control group. This is confirmed by Lipsey (1992) who found that control groups that received some attention (which is common practice in juvenile justice settings) showed less contrast with treatment groups than where control groups received no treatment of any kind.

Finally, critics of meta-analysis have warned that it is unsafe to assume that the reports of programmes included in the analysis are representative of all similar programmes. This is because studies yielding positive results are more likely to be published and hence available to meta-analysts. Some meta-analysts (Lipsey, 1992; Redondo et al., 1996) have sought to overcome this problem by broadening the coverage of the literature to include both published and unpublished reports. Redondo found, moreover, that there were no significant differences between the unpublished and the published studies in terms of the effectiveness of the programmes included. It must be acknowledged, moreover, that publication bias is also a feature of orthodox literature reviews.

Given the limitations in the primary studies on which meta-analytic reviews are based and the above qualifications regarding the use of this technique as a means of quantifying differences between offender programmes, what can be gleaned from the research literature about the effectiveness of cognitive-behavioural techniques? If there is evidence to suggest this approach is significantly more effective than others, what, if anything, does the literature reveal about the main forms of successful cognitive-behavioural intervention with different types of offender, such as those convicted of sex or violent offences or involved in drug abuse? This section considers the available evidence with a view to clarifying what conclusions it is safe to draw and which claims should be treated with a degree of caution.

The use and effectiveness of cognitive-behavioural approaches with offenders

Since the most extensive and recent meta-analyses have focused wholly or primarily on juveniles and young offender programmes, the findings reported in this overview regarding interventions with adult offenders are limited. As will also be apparent, the majority of the original studies were undertaken in North America in the 1970s and 1980s. Unsurprisingly, therefore, some commentators have expressed considerable scepticism about the applicability of the results and conclusions to adult offenders sentenced in this country (Mair, 1995; Losel, 1993). In fact, Losel et al. (1987), Mayer et al. (1986) and Lipsey (1992) found no significant relationship between age and treatment effect in their meta-analyses. Since, however, the age range for most studies included ended at 21, this will have effectively excluded many offenders with serious drug and alcohol problems which have developed over time or with long-standing relationship or employment difficulties. These kinds of personal factors can be expected to have a bearing on programme success irrespective of the programme content and approach. Despite this, in one of the largest meta-analyses to have included juvenile and adult offender programmes Andrews et al. (1990) found no significant difference in their effectiveness according to age. And, as will be seen, certain of the factors identified in meta-analytic reviews as being associated with successful outcomes have been confirmed by the results of individual studies with adults (e.g. Ross et al., 1988) and by the work with sex offenders.

The first part of this section summarises the findings of individual studies or meta-analyses which are not focused upon any particular type of offence. The age category or categories encompassed are mentioned where this is known, together with any recorded differences in the effectiveness of cognitive-behavioural approaches according to the age of the offenders. The following sub-sections consider the use and impact of cognitive-behavioural interventions with alcohol and drug abusing, violent and sexual offenders.

Juvenile and adult offenders

Individual studies have produced conflicting results about which forms of behavioural and cognitive-behavioural work are most effective with juveniles and young offenders. Hollin (1990, 1993, 1996) and McGuire (1996a) reviewed a wide range of studies and concluded that interventions based solely on social skills training (e.g. Klein et al., 1977) have had limited success while those based solely on individual behaviour therapy have sometimes been successful but are unpopular with young offenders. Approaches which combine behavioural techniques with social learning and cognition, including teaching young offenders self-control, appear to be the most promising in reducing reoffending. For example, Feindler and Ecton (1986) developed a programme for young offenders which successfully taught them how to control anger, while McDougall et al. (1987) reported significant anger reductions among inmates in young offenders' institutions who had undergone an anger management programme combining cognitive procedures, specifically self-instruction and self-statements to use in situations of anger, with role playing to improve behavioural responses and an educational module to help offenders understand their anger. The sample size in the McDougall study was small (n=18) and the measurement of effectiveness was limited to a comparison between treatment and controls in the use of Governor's reports three months after completion of the programme. Lochman (1992), moreover, assessed a similar programme in a school and found that, although self-esteem and social problem solving skills were increased, there was no long-term impact on recidivism.

A study by Borduin et al. (1995) examined the long-term effectiveness of 'multi systemic therapy' (MST), an approach which directly addresses personal (including cognitive) and social (family, peer group and school) factors that are believed to be associated with adolescent antisocial behaviour. A sample of 176 families with a juvenile offender (aged 12–17) were randomly assigned to MST and conventional individual therapy (IT). All of the offenders had records of serious criminal involvement. Following therapy the two groups were compared on a number of measures related to the goals of improving individual adjustment and family relations and reducing involvement in criminal activity. On all outcome measures the MST group showed significant improvements which were not reported in respect of the control group. At the end of the four year follow-up the overall arrest rate for MST completers (22%) was less than one - third the rate for the individual therapy group (71%). Those who dropped out of MST were at higher risk of arrest (47%) than those who completed but were still at lower risk than those who underwent IT. MST was also associated with significantly fewer serious crimes among those who were arrested.

Bourdin et al. consider that the success of MST with high risk young offenders may be due to its recognition of the multiple determinants of antisocial behaviour and its explicit focus on ameliorating behavioural problems within the context of problematic family relations.

Turning to the findings from meta-analyses of programmes which have been undertaken with juveniles and young offenders, Losel (1993, 1995) has estimated an overall effect size of 0.20 for all the meta-analyses he considered, which means that recidivism for treatment groups was 10 per cent less than for the control groups. Programmes that yielded the best results were "cognitive-behavioural, skills orientated and multimodal". Similarly, Palmer (1994) found that approaches classified as behavioural were among the most successful with juveniles (i.e., had the largest average effect sizes or reductions in recidivism when comparing experimental and control groups). Programmes that used cognitive-behavioural, or combinations of cognitive and life skills approaches also showed success–though often under other labels such as 'social skills training'–as did those simply classified as multimodal. Palmer reports that the least effective approaches are those which employ confrontation, group counselling/therapy (unless carefully focused), and individual counselling/therapy.

Lipsey's review of published and unpublished research concerning 443 programmes for juvenile offenders has been influential because it is one of the most systematic and rigorous to date (Lipsey 1992, 1995; Palmer, 1994). Lipsey's sample included offenders in the 12–21 age range, although most were aged 18. For 285 (64%) of the programmes recidivism was lower for the treatment groups. Even more important was the finding that in 131 (30%) studies treatment programmes actually *increased* delinquency. These were punishment or deterrence based interventions, such as shock incarceration and boot camps, which provided little by way of education, training or therapy. Having controlled for factors such as the different measures used by each study to judge recidivism (e.g. arrest, conviction etc.) and the type of research design (randomised or non-randomised treatment and control groups), Lipsey concluded that programmes which were multi modal and had a more concrete, behavioural or "skills-oriented" character had the most impact both within and outside the juvenile justice system with effect sizes of 0.20–0.32 (equivalent to a 10–16% reduction in recidivism against untreated controls). Lipsey did not attempt to disentangle the ingredients of successful multi modal packages and cautioned that the "inherent fuzziness of these coded categories" makes futile any discussion of whether particular forms of intervention are *universally* superior to others, (Lipsey, in McGuire, 1995 ed). Like Palmer, however, Lipsey found that concrete, structured approaches focused directly on overt behaviour, were more successful than were traditional counselling and casework techniques.

An earlier meta-analysis by Whitehead and Lab (1989) is notable for the fact that the authors reached more pessimistic conclusions about the success of rehabilitative work with juveniles than in subsequent meta-analyses. On the basis of an analysis of 50 programmes for juvenile offenders Whitehead and Lab found that only 24–32 per cent of programmes were successful in terms of achieving significant reductions in recidivism. They concluded that no single type of intervention "displayed overwhelmingly positive results on recidivism". It should be noted, however, that of the 50 studies in the meta-analysis, 30 involved juvenile diversion, which may not have included any form of intervention intended to address offending behaviour. Previous studies have indicated that diversionary approaches, which tend not to be used with relatively serious offenders, produce smaller effect sizes than other forms of intervention, perhaps because the offenders are judged to be fairly good risks in the first place.

This finding is generally considered to be a consequence of the researchers' use of very strict criteria for success that would require large reductions in recidivism, not simply a statistically significant difference between experimental and control groups. The equivalent effect sizes were larger than those noted in other meta-analyses (Palmer, 1994; Losel, 1995; Farrington, 1996). When Andrews and colleagues (1990) re-analysed 45 of the 50 studies considered by Whitehead and Lab and included a further 35 studies (a third of which covered programmes for adult offenders) their conclusions were more in line with those reached by Losel, Lipsey and others. The authors speculate that effect sizes may have risen throughout the 1980s precisely because of the increasing use of cognitive methods within behavioural programmes.

Drawing on the findings of previous studies, Andrews et al. differentiated between 'appropriate' and 'inappropriate' services. Appropriate services were defined as those which delivered more intensive treatment to higher risk offenders; targetted the criminogenic needs associated with offending; and used cognitive or behavioural approaches. Inappropriate services were those which delivered treatment to low risk offenders, or failed to match the teaching styles of staff to offenders' learning styles; or used group approaches with no specific aims (Palmer, 1994). For appropriate programmes recidivism rates were on average 53 per cent lower than for inappropriate services. Andrews et al., like Lipsey, also reported increased recidivism rates where the intervention was intended to punish or deter rather than to rehabilitate through appropriate service.

Although Whitehead and Lab were critical of Andrews et al. analysis and conclusions regarding appropriate correctional approaches (Lab and Whitehead, 1990), in a rejoinder Andrews et al. (1990a) re-asserted that their empirical findings were robust and reliable. They conceded, however, that Whitehead and Lab were correct in noting the need for further research to support the theory that the connection between treatment and recidivism is mediated by change in criminogenic factors. In other words, there is a need for more research *"...on the links among treatment, intermediate change and recidivism".*

Izzo and Ross's (1990) analysis of 46 juvenile offender studies conducted during the period 1970–1985 also indicated that programmes which incorporate a cognitive component were more than twice as effective as those which did not, again, using effect size as a measure of the difference between experimental and control groups. Izzo and Ross described the individual cognitive programmes as using one or more of the following:

problem solving; negotiation skills training; interpersonal skills training; rational-emotive therapy; role-playing and modelling; or cognitive-behavioural modification. Effective programmes targetted not only the offender's cognition, self-evaluation, expectations and values, but his or her behaviour and vocational or interpersonal skills.

A review carried out by Antonowicz and Ross (1994) was confined to studies of adults and juveniles published between 1970 and 1991 which utilised experimental or quasi-experimental designs and which included a community based follow-up (including reconviction rates).[1] Their focus on well designed and controlled studies meant that only 44 published reports fitted their qualifying criteria. Chi-square tests were used to test the differences in recidivism between treatment and control groups. Successful programmes were characterised by a sound conceptual model; a focus upon criminogenic needs; responsiveness to offenders' learning styles (using role play and modelling); and the use of cognitive skills training. Programmes containing these elements comprised 75 per cent (15/20) of successful programmes compared with 38 per cent (9/24) of those which were unsuccessful. Programmes based on deterrence or psychodynamic methods were unsuccessful in demonstrating a statistically significant improvement in recidivism when compared with the control groups. Behaviourally-orientated programs that did not include a cognitive component were also unsuccessful.

Antonowicz and Ross differentiated between cognitive therapy or cognitive-behavioural modification (designed to modify *what* an offender thinks) and cognitive skills training (designed to teach an offender *how* to think). They concluded from the studies examined that cognitive skills training should precede attempts to modify what they think. While Antonowicz and Ross could not say which particular cognitive skills methods were most successful, they did show that the following were more prevalent in successful than in unsuccessful programmes: training in social perspective taking; training in self-control; interpersonal problem solving; and values enhancement (a form of moral education).

A cognitive skills based programme which has been used in a variety of different settings in Canada, Mexico and Europe is the Reasoning and Rehabilitation (R and R) programme developed by Robert Ross and colleagues (Ross et al. 1989). This is an intensive cognitive skills programme for high risk offenders, based on a long-term research project that included a review of the literature published over the previous 40 years and an analysis

---

1   The study was not strictly a meta-analysis as the 44 studies were not combined to produce an overall treatment effect and to discover key characteristics; rather Antonowicz and Ross selected success criteria from earlier studies and calculated the proportion of successful and unsuccessful ones which contained these characteristics.

of offender rehabilitation programmes. The research indicated that effective programmes included an intervention technique which could influence cognitive deficits whereas ineffective programmes did not. This suggested to the researchers that cognitive skills training is a key element in any successful programme. The programme is multimodal in that it is designed to modify many aspects of offenders thinking, including egocentricity, impulsiveness, and failure to understand the views and feelings of others.[2] More details can be found in the Reasoning and Rehabilitation handbook (Ross et al. 1989).

In 1988 the R & R programme, which consists of 80 hours of intensive training delivered to groups of four-six offenders by five specially trained probation officers, was first piloted in Ontario, Canada. Offenders were randomly assigned to a control group of regular probationers (n=23); a group of regular probationers given additional life skills training (n=17); and to the Reasoning and Rehabilitation group (n=22). The average age of the offenders was 24. All members of the sample had similar levels of risk (calculated through use of the Level of Supervision Inventory or LSI), although the R & R group had slightly more previous convictions. The nine-month reconviction results were very impressive as only 18 per cent of the R & R group were reconvicted compared with 69 per cent of regular probationers and 47 per cent of the life skills group.

Although the results are favourable, the sample sizes for each group are small and the follow up period (9 months) is short. Nonetheless, the programme has been widely adopted across North America and Spain and is on the core curriculum for the Correctional Services of Canada (CSC) which includes 47 prisons and community residencies across Canada (Ross & Ross ed., 1996).

By late 1993 programmes based on Reasoning and Rehabilitation had been developed by 13 probation areas in England and Wales. In most areas evaluation has only been carried out via client feedback (McGuire, 1995a), the exception being the programme implemented in 1991 by the Mid-Glamorgan probation service entitled 'STOP' - *Straight Thinking On Probation*. STOP comprises 35 intensive sessions based on the R & R programme. To date, over 150 offenders have received STOP orders from courts (Raynor & Vanstone 1996, Knott 1995) and their performance on the project has been subjected to independent evaluation.

The research design consisted of comparing the patterns of reconviction for a group of offenders attending STOP with that of comparison groups subject

---

2   The full list, from Ross et al. (1988), is: structured learning theory (to teach social skills); lateral thinking (to teach creative problem solving); critical thinking (to teach logical, rational thinking); values education (to teach values, concern for others); assertiveness training (to teach non-aggressive ways to meet ends); negotiation skills training (to teach alternatives to violent behaviours in interpersonal conflict situations); interpersonal cognitive problem solving (to teach thinking skills required to deal with interpersonal problems and conflicts); social perspective training (to recognise and understand other people's views and feelings); and role-playing and modelling (to demonstrate socially acceptable behaviours).

to: standard probation orders; probation orders with day centre requirements; community service orders; immediate custody of up to 12 months; and suspended sentences. For each group predicted risk of reconviction scores were also calculated. These scores enabled Raynor and Vanstone (1994, 1996) to assess how each group fared compared with their expected reconviction scores.

After 12 months the reconviction rate for those who completed the STOP programme was better than predicted (35% compared with 42% predicted). This pattern was not evident for the comparison groups. For example, 49 per cent of the custodial group were reconvicted compared with a predicted rate of 42 per cent. However, the results were not sustained in the second year when 63 per cent of STOP completers were reconvicted (against a predicted rate of 61%) (Raynor and Vanstone, 1996).

Raynor and Vanstone also noted that after 12 months only five (8%) of the 59 STOP completers has been reconvicted of a serious offence (violent/sexual offences or burglary) compared with 34 (21%) of those given custody and 19 (18%) of those sentenced to STOP but who did not complete the programme. Again, these differences were not sustained in the second year: after 24 months the percentages reconvicted for serious offences for the STOP full sample, custody and STOP completers were 27 per cent, 25 per cent and 22 per cent respectively. However, the STOP completers were still more likely to avoid prison when reconvicted, which Raynor and Vanstone believe may reflect a lesser degree of seriousness than simple offence codes indicate. Raynor and Vanstone consider that better results, both in terms of longer term outcome and completions, could be achieved by more appropriate offender selection, by offering support and follow-up to offenders who complete the programme and by applying the 'reasoning and rehabilitation' model outside the actual group sessions.

A recent British study of five probation run group programmes for adult offenders investigated their short-term effectiveness in achieving their stated aims and attempted to identify the links between process characteristics, e.g. integrity, coherent aims etc., and eventual outcome, as measured by pre and post treatment assessment (McGuire et al., 1995). The five programmes considered were: a seven - week programme for drink driving offenders; a structured activity programme for motoring offenders; a day centre activity programme of the type used by many probation services; a cognitive skills training package based on the 'Reasoning and Rehabilitation' programme; and a group for women offenders. The drink driving programme, the cognitive skills programme and the programme for women offenders all used cognitive-behavioural methods to some degree.

The short timescale of the study did not permit examination of reconviction rates following completion of the programme but a number of other measures were used including a range of pre/post treatment psychological tests, the crime-pics risk of reoffending questionnaire and the Rosenbury self-esteem scale. There were other tests specific to each programme (e.g. alcohol knowledge tests, driving behaviour etc.). The cognitive skills programme was assessed via six additional tests which measured alternative thinking, impulsiveness and locus of control (the degree to which offenders perceive events to be out of their control). Comparison groups were selected among offenders who had been recommended for placement on the programmes but who received other disposals (mostly custodial sentences or community service orders).

The results of this programme were mixed. Only the drink driving programme achieved statistically significant pre and post test differences on the various tests, while no significant differences were detected in the comparison group. Other programmes, including the course on cognitive training, showed promising, but non-significant results. The authors believe that the failure to demonstrate statistically significant improvement could be a function of the small number of offenders (a total of 65 offenders across the five programmes) and the dearth of standardised tests for evaluating these types of intervention. In addition, some of the programmes lacked one or more of the features described above which meta-analysts have identified as distinguishing the more successful offender programmes. Whereas the drink driving programme incorporated all the success factors, the cognitive training programme lacked specific targetting and programme integrity (or at least these requirements were not evident in the questionnaire responses). The women offenders group used cognitive-behavioural methods and had a directive style of working but lacked programme integrity, had no clear aims or specific treatment targets, and was not highly structured. The day centre programme had a directive approach but lacked any of the other success criteria.

Despite the inconclusive findings from this study, the researchers consider that they lend support to the conclusions of large scale meta-analyses regarding the combination of ingredients which yield the most promising results with high, or relatively high risk offenders.

To summarise this subsection, the available research on juvenile and adult offender programmes points to a broad consensus as to the types of approach which achieve the greatest impact on offending behaviour (expressed in terms of experimental studies achieving lower recidivism rates than controls). Those which combine cognitive-behavioural techniques with the other success factors identified in the meta-analysis (targetting, structured approaches, programme integrity) appear to offer the best chance of reducing rates of recidivism. Although the findings are limited with regard to adult offenders, the message with regard to cognitive-behavioural approaches is consistent with that reported in the more numerous studies of young offenders. The reviews by Lipsey (1992) and Andrews et al. (1990) also indicate that, while some forms of intervention are associated with fairly large reductions in recidivism, those based on the use of punitive measures actually appear to increase the chances of reoffending.

As Lipsey (1995) concludes, however, only general and broad brush advice on effective interventions is possible on the basis of meta-analyses which aggregate over a wide range of studies. All interventions must be developed and delivered in accordance with the particular needs and circumstances of the offender. This is consistent with Palmer's (1994) observation that "which particular combinations of experimental program features have commonly yielded positive results with large portions of their populations – and which have not–has seldom been systematically explored and is largely unknown". Moreover, in order to make progress in determining which particular forms of cognitive-behavioural training and combinations seem promising, Palmer stresses that researchers and others need first to develop and agree definitions for the various components of any given combination.

In short, although the simple, brief labels typically allocated to programmes do not permit "fine grain reporting" of the components associated with reduced recidivism, Lipsey and others find sufficient evidence in the pattern of results to permit some broad inferences. The consistently strong effect of multimodal combinations reported in several meta-analyses does suggest that there may be advantage, having assessed an offender's criminogenic needs, in seeking to address them within a single, integrated programme.

Substance abusers

Once again evaluation of programmes delivered to drug abusing offenders has, in the main, been conducted in North America. In a review of the literature of drug misuse and the criminal justice system Hough (1995) points out that these reviews have largely been of programmes rather than programme components–a general difficulty with the literature concerning rehabilitative work with offenders. Moreover, many studies of different forms of treatment have not evaluated programmes located within the criminal justice system and have not examined effectiveness in reducing reoffending. For example, a review carried out by Husband and Platt (1993) of approaches used to address drug and alcohol abuse indicates that cognitive skills approaches which include problem solving training are successful in reducing alcohol intake. The review does not examine whether this type of approach was also effective in reducing further offending, but an evaluation by Platt, Perry and Metzger (1980) on a heroin treatment programme which included behavioural therapy and training in interpersonal problem-solving showed promising results with regard to reoffending. Young offenders who attended the programme, which was located within a youth correctional centre, had significantly lower rates of parole revocation for further offences (both drug and non-drug offences) than a matched control group. One other published study, reported by Johnson and Hunter (1995) examined patterns of parole revocation for groups of drug abusing offenders, some of whom attended a programme adapted from the Ross et al. R & R programme. Drug offenders were randomly assigned to either regular probation, a non-cognitive drug programme or the cognitive skills programme. After one year 6/32 (19%) of the cognitive sample had been revoked, compared with 8/23 (35%) for the regular probation and 10/33 (30%) of the non-cognitive drug programme. With such small numbers, however, these results are not statistically significant.

An approach advocated by McMurran and Hollin (1993) for addressing substance abuse is that of a modular programme involving: thorough assessment; behavioural social skills training (BSCT); skills training; relapse prevention; and lifestyle modification. According to this approach the client acts as a '*personal scientist*', monitoring alcohol consumption, setting goals, and modifying his or her expectations from alcohol consumption. BSCT has been successful in reducing alcohol consumption in non-offender populations, but again, there is no evidence of its effect on recidivism in offender populations. Furthermore, the approach has apparently not been attempted with illicit drugs users (McMurran, 1996). McMurran's (1996) review of the literature on alcohol, drugs and crime also confirmed that there is insufficient research evidence to permit conclusions about precisely what combinations of cognitive, behavioural and skills elements are necessary for successful intervention, measured in terms of both substance intake reduction and in reduced recidivism. This is unsurprising, given the complexity of the research task and the relatively few studies in this field of enquiry.

While programmes such as methadone maintenance and detoxification focus on the immediate need to treat the addiction, relapse prevention techniques are, as the label suggests, concerned with longer term coping strategies and with enabling drug misusing offenders to recognise situations where there is a high risk of a recurrence of the problem behaviour. Cognitive-behavioural approaches are used in relapse prevention, techniques including role playing of high risk situations, positive self-statements etc. There is some evidence of their success in alcohol treatment groups: Allsop and Saunders (1989) found that offenders who underwent relapse prevention were less likely to relapse to heavy drinking after 6 months. However, as far as we are aware, there is no published evidence of the success of relapse prevention techniques with drug users nor of their impact on recidivism among substance abusing offenders.

Violent offenders

There is a growing body of research evidence which links aggressive and violent behaviour with early family experiences, in particular poor child rearing and parenting, harsh and authoritarian discipline. Cohort studies, such as that undertaken by Farrington (1996) indicate that the roots of aggression and violence, like other forms of anti-social behaviour, are learned, and that the family plays a key role in determining whether early patterns of aggressive behaviour become established. While not denying the importance of early environmental and socialisation factors, in order to improve the effectiveness of interventions with those whose aggressive behaviour has become established, psychologists have also sought a fuller understanding of the cognitive processes which underlie and trigger this form of behaviour.

One of the most prolific researchers in the area of violent offending has been Novaco (1975, 1978). Novaco describes anger as being caused by a physiological arousal which is then labelled by an offender, the labelling being dependant on how an offender perceives his or her social or environmental situation. Hence, "*it is suggested that cognitive restructuring of a violent person's perception of social events, and their relationships with others, can help in reducing aggressive behaviour and hostility*" (Brown and Howells, 1996). Where cognitive techniques are used with violent offenders these would normally follow Novaco's approach (Blackburn, 1995). This combines the use of cognitive self-control with relaxation techniques and an educational element to help offenders understand their behaviour. Novaco found that the self-control element combined with relaxation had a greater impact on anger than relaxation alone. Later research by Schlicter (1978) confirmed that a combination of relaxation training with self-instructional methods of anger control and 'coping skills' had a greater impact on aggressive adolescents than basic group counselling. Feindler and Ecton (1986) also obtained promising results with aggressive adolescents when using cognitive-behavioural techniques in a programme of anger-control and social skills training.

Glick and Goldstein (1987) reviewed and evaluated many of these techniques in developing their Aggression Replacement Training (ART) for young violent offenders, which has been adapted for use with violent young adults. The combination of anger control training techniques (based in part on Novaco's work) with social skills training, problem solving and moral education has been found to improve self-control and there is some evidence of a reduction in recidivism (e.g., Leeman, Gibbs and Fuller, 1993).

However, whether programmes such as ART can significantly reduce the rate of violent offending is uncertain. One study found that the beneficial effect failed to reach statistical significance once allowance was made for differences in levels of supervision received by the treatment and control group following the programme (Glick et al. 1989).

The influence of the family upon adolescent antisocial and aggressive behaviour has led some psychologists to involve the family in therapy through the use of cognitive skills training and problem solving methods. In the study reported by Borduin et al. (1995) on the effectiveness of 'multi systemic treatment' (which addressed behaviour problems in the context of family, peer group and school), offenders aged 12–17 were randomly assigned to multisystemic treatment (MST) or individual therapy. Outcome measures included arrests for violent crimes (rape, attempted rape, aggravated assault etc.) during a four year follow-up. The youths who participated in MST, many of whom had previously committed offences of violence, were significantly less likely to be arrested for further violent crimes than were youths who received individual therapy. The researchers concluded from this finding that interventions with violent young offenders are likely to be more effective if they are comprehensive, address behavioural problems within the context of problematic family relations, and are delivered in the family's home or at a community location.

Some evidence that cognitive-behavioural work with violent adult offenders can reduce reoffending has emerged from a recent evaluation funded by the Scottish Office and Home Office of two re-education programmes for perpetrators of domestic violence (Dobash et al. 1996). Both programmes adopted a cognitive-behavioural approach and consisted of weekly group sessions over a six to seven month period. The aim was to increase the offenders' insight into their violent behaviour and to model new ways of thinking and acting through the use of a range of behavioural and cognitive techniques. These included: teaching cognitive techniques for recognising the sequence of events and the emotions associated with the on-set of violence; use of continuous forms of self-assessment and monitoring as a means of reinforcing group work; practising new behaviour through role play; and didactic methods to enhance offenders' understanding of the nature of violent behaviour towards women.

In order to assess the effectiveness of these two programmes the study followed up two groups of men who participated in the programmes (a total of 41 men) and compared them with a group of 71 men who received other court disposals. Reoffending by the programme and other court disposal group was assessed by interviewing women partners three and 12 months after the completion of the programme, thus significantly reducing the effect of undetected offending inherent in most reconviction studies. The research could not control for the effects of selection either by Sheriffs or by programme staff and although there was no statistical difference between the programme and control groups in terms of the men's use of violence, there were a few differences between them in their ages, employment status and background of parental violence. Bearing in mind that the sample was quite small and may have been subject to some selection bias, the results are viewed by the researchers as encouraging. Only 33 per cent of those who participated in the programme had committed a violent act against their partners after 12 months, compared with 75 per cent of those who received other criminal justice disposals. Women whose partners did undergo treatment also noted reductions in the coercive and controlling behaviour known to be associated with domestic violence, such as threats, shouting and restrictions on the women's social life.

On the basis of an examination of the use of behavioural and cognitive techniques with violent offenders, Blackburn (1995) concluded that training in anger management has indeed been shown to reduce aggression, at least in the short term, and its usefulness in maintaining order in institutions has been established. However, evidence of long term success is inconclusive, particularly for the more persistent violent offenders who may require more intensive interventions. Hence Blackburn's observation in relation to violent offenders that *"issues such as offender heterogeneity, effective treatment components and treatment intensity have yet to be addressed"* (Blackburn, 1995, p382).

Sex offenders

Cognitive-behavioural methods with sex offenders attempt to modify three sets of problems: deviant sexuality, social competence and attitudinal/cognitive distortions (Epps, 1996). Deviant sexuality is tackled through behavioural methods such as aversion therapy, where deviant desires are associated with unpleasant consequences. Social competence training includes improving empathy and assertiveness, anger management, communication and conflict resolution. Techniques used include problem solving and social skills training. Attitudinal and cognitive distortions can be addressed using group discussions, for example, where each offender is videoed talking about his or her offending behaviour which is then discussed by members of the group (Epps, 1996; Barker and Morgan, 1993).

Evidence of the impact of these techniques has mainly come from the US Furby et al. (1989) reviewed studies which included recidivism as a measure but found little evidence of success. This may, however, have been due to poor research designs, which prevented any firm conclusions being reached (Marques, 1994), and to the low rates of reconvictions by sex offenders in the non-treatment control groups. For example, Marshall and Barberee's (1990) review of the outcome of cognitive-behavioural treatment programmes with sex offenders includes only one study in which outcome results are shown for both treated and untreated groups. The results of some studies are also qualified by the high drop out rates from the programmes which may have exaggerated their success in reducing recidivism. These methodological weaknesses may account in part for the number of unexplained inconsistencies noted by Marshall and Barberee and their conclusion that better indices of treatment effectiveness are required, including detailed information on changes in sexual preferences, social competence and cognitive distortions.

An American study which does include a control group and is based on a reasonable sample size and incorporates a long term follow up is the Californian Sex Offender Treatment Evaluation Program (SOTEP). The results of this longitudinal study of reoffending rates for offenders who attended the programme have recently been published (Marques, 1994). SOTEP uses a multi modal approach which includes social skills training and drug/alcohol treatment according to offender needs and a cognitive-behavioural dimension which focuses on relapse prevention, providing offenders with sufficient controls to anticipate and avoid future risk situations. The programme is delivered in hospital and is followed by one year's community follow-up with much emphasis of relapse prevention when offenders are released. The research design included a treatment group of 98 offenders, a "volunteer" control group of 97 offenders (who volunteered for, but did not receive, treatment) and a "non-volunteer" control group of 96 offenders (who refused the opportunity to receive treatment). Treated offenders have been at risk (i.e. free to reoffend) for different periods of time–ranging from three months to six and a half years with an average of just under three years. So far the treatment group has had the least number of reconvictions, but the researchers note that data collection will need to continue until the end of this decade in order to achieve a large enough sample with adequate time at risk to detect statistical differences in reoffending rates.

In England and Wales, both prison and probation services run cognitive-behavioural programmes for sex offenders. A recent ACOP survey (Proctor and Flaxington, 1996) showed that 7,109 sex offenders were being supervised by the probation service during the summer of 1995, half of whom were in prison. The service has provision to send 1,907 offenders through treatment centres each year. Between 1991 and 1995 the number of individual offender programmes grew from 63 to 109; only seven services had no such provision.

In 1991 the Home Office commissioned a team of forensic clinical psychologists to evaluate seven community-based treatment programmes for sex offenders (Beckett et al. 1994). The selected programmes included one long-term residential cognitive-behavioural programme and six programmes run by probation services. Pre and post treatment deviancy were assessed via a battery of psychological tests designed to measure changes in factors believed to contribute towards reoffending. The long-term residential centre was more successful than short-term programmes in treating both low and high deviancy men. Following therapy a treatment effect was identified for 60 per cent of high deviancy offenders, including a greater admittance of offending behaviour and improvements in self esteem and assertiveness. The shorter probation run programmes had less success with both high and medium deviancy offenders. There were, however, some signs that a significant minority of the offenders (25%) showed less empathy towards their victims after treatment than before, possibly because work on victim empathy was introduced too early in the therapy. Two-year reconviction rates, calculated for 134 of the STEP offenders (Hedderman and Sugg, 1996), show that none of the 24 offenders whose scores on the psychometric tests indicated a significant response to treatment had been reconvicted within this period.

Designing and delivering effective programmes

A recurring theme within the literature reviewed in this report is the importance of targetting interventions to meet the needs of individual offenders and delivering programmes in a manner which matches offenders' learning styles. Thus, although multi modal programming gains support in studies of interventions with juvenile and adult offenders, this approach can only work if each element of the programme explicitly addresses the particular needs of the individual offender and those responsible for assessment and allocation avoid a *'blunderbuss approach'* (McGuire, 1995a, p278), where offenders are bombarded with every available course module in the hope that some of it will have an impact. If, moreover, programmes are designed to address a wide range of criminogenic needs, an approach which the research suggests is much favoured, it is important to ensure that those selected to attend the various components are assessed as likely to be receptive to both the content and style of delivery.

Unfortunately, the findings from meta-analytic studies leave a number of questions unanswered with regard to the relative importance of the different components of programmes which appear to be effective, the criteria for assessing need and the theories which should guide the process of matching offenders to programme content and mode of delivery. As McGuire points out (McGuire, 1995 ed., p 25) the fact that the existing evidence favours programmes with a number of components makes this type of research problematic but of considerable importance if progress is to be made in translating broad principles into practice.

Assessing need and matching offenders to programmes

Burnett's (1996) study of assessment and allocation procedures within the probation service indicates that current systems for assessing offending related needs and matching offenders to programmes is often unsatisfactory. There was evidence of under-use of group programmes, such as offending behaviour groups, because probation staff viewed them as 'packaged' and impersonal or too broad to be of relevance to offenders, with no readily identified content. A related problem was that the offence types and offenders included in programmes were too diverse for their needs to be adequately addressed in a group setting. More needed to be done, it was felt, to focus on the criminogenic needs of individual offenders.

One way of improving the assessment process and of ensuring such a focus, is through the use of standard assessment scales which include the full range of problems considered to be related to offending behaviour. As Aubrey and Hough (1997) point out, the best examples of statistically derived diagnostic scales currently used within the probation service are concerned with predicting the risk of reconviction rather than assessing needs. These scales have concentrated on static indicators which have been shown to be statistically related to reconviction (type of offence, age, sex and previous offending) although some include selected psychological indictors.

An assessment tool developed by Hare (1980) known as the Psychopathy Checklist (revised to a 20-item version, the PCL-R), is an example of a scale devised by clinical psychologists which successfully combines static and dynamic factors which correlate with psychopathy and have strong predictive power with respect to recidivism among psychopaths. The PCL-R (and the shorter screening version, PCL:SV) has been shown to be a robust predictor of further offending by psychopaths. By combining demographic, criminogenic and psychological information (including poor behavioural control, impulsiveness, frequent marital failure and a history of juvenile delinquency) PCL-R challenges the view that dynamic factors add little to the predictive power of static factors (Hollin and Palmer 1995).[3] As Cooke (1996) points out, however, the majority of published studies on use of PCL-R have been carried out in North America. When PCL-R ratings were obtained by Cooke from a sample of Scottish prisoners the prevalence of

---

3   The full list is: superficial charm; grandiose sense of self-worth; need for stimulation/easily bored; pathological lying; manipulative; lack of remorse or guilt; no emotional depth; callous; parasitic lifestyle; poor behavioural control; promiscuous sexual behaviour; early behavioural problems; lack of long-term planning; impulsive; irresponsible; failure to accept responsibility for own actions; delinquent as a juvenile; poor record on probation or other conditional release; versatile as a criminal (Hare 1991).

psychopathy was found to be substantially lower than among North American prisoners, suggesting that the scale may have limited application in this country.

Of particular relevance to cognitive skills work (also recommended by Hollin and Palmer for use within the Prison Service), is the Psychological Inventory of Criminal Thinking Styles (PICTS), an 80 item questionnaire evaluating 10 cognitive deficits.[4] PICTS has recently been piloted on 450 federal prison inmates in the USA and successfully differentiated between maximum, medium and low security inmates (Walters, 1995).

In a review of research on the assessment and management of risk and dangerousness, Kemshall (1996) considers that the predictive accuracy of risk assessment scales can be enhanced by including dynamic and situationally specific factors which permit an assessment of change in risk over time. Kemshall cautions, however, that actuarial assessments (those based on statistical analysis of data derived from sample groups of the population), have inherent limitations and need to be applied with care. She concludes that a combination of actuarial and clinical assessment offers the most productive way forward for the probation service. The scope for improving the accuracy of reconviction scales by including a range of social variables (including marital status, drug/alcohol use and employment) is shortly to be examined in a Home Office study.

Although statistically-based needs scales are less developed than reconviction scales within the probation service there are a number of examples of American and Canadian scales in which offending-related needs are assessed in conjunction with risk. A scale which combines needs and risks within one score, the Level of Service Inventory-Revised (LSI-R), has been in use in Canada for some years and is currently attracting considerable interest in this country (Andrews, 1982; Andrews and Bonta, 1995). The LSI-R is based on social learning theory and was developed specifically with treatment planning and supervision in mind. Extensively validated in Canada, the LSI-R has ten sub components: criminal history; education/employment; financial; family/marital; accommodation; leisure/recreation; companions; alcohol/drug problems; emotional/personal; and attitudes/motivation. The revised version, contains specific criteria for planning probation supervision, assessing likely recidivism and identifying treatment targets (Andrews and Bonta, 1995; Hollin and Palmer, 1995). This scale is currently being piloted in several probation services in England and Wales and in selected adult prisons and Young Offenders Institutions.

There is some evidence that the growth of allocation and assessment

---

4   The full list is confusion; defensiveness; mollification; cutoff; entitlement; power orientation; sentimentality; super-optimism; cognitive indolence and discontinuity (Walters, 1995).

instruments might meet resistance from some officers who feel they are being 'de-skilled'. A recent study of the use of similar risk/needs instruments in probation supervision decisions in the US indicated that some officers felt their professionalism was being undermined by these scales (Schneider et al. 1996). Others, however, believed that such instruments eliminated the arbitrary nature of decisions made. And as Burnett (1996) has argued:

> "A more systematic assessment of offending-related needs will enhance the accuracy and status of probation assessments...and would facilitate integrated evaluation of the effectiveness of community supervision".

Programme integrity

There is an increasing body of research evidence that interventions with offenders may fail through lack of adherence to the agreed objectives and procedures. Hollin (1995) isolates three basic threats to programme integrity and discusses the implications for the delivery and evaluation of programmes.

- *programme drift* as characterised by a gradual shift over time in its aims. Johnson (1981) illustrates how, for example, as a result of lack of management and the *'immediacy of routine tasks'* a psychodynamic programme for offenders changed from an emphasis on therapeutic issues to a concern for routine administration.

- *programme reversal* occurs when staff work to undermine the goals of the programme. Hollin cites an example from Schlichter and Horan (1981) where staff on an anger management programme designed to encourage self-control believed the problem was, in fact, one of 'pent-up anger' which needed to be expressed. Their theoretical perspective thus differed radically from the perspective of those who designed the programme.

- *programme of non-compliance* occurs when practitioners omit or modify elements of the programme. For example, certain sessions could be dropped and others added, particularly when a programme is 'handed down' via in-service training, which Hollin compares with a game of 'Chinese whispers'.

It must be acknowledged, however, that modifications may be necessary in order to meet offenders' needs, especially where programmes are 'bought-in' from different criminal justice systems (Ross and Ross, 1995). .For example, in his study of 'Reasoning and Rehabilitation' programmes in the UK,

McGuire (1995a) discusses some implications of the cultural differences between North America and the UK. At a superficial level, there were problems caused by the use of American terminology and colloquialisms; more fundamentally, the North American course material made assumptions regarding offenders' willingness to contribute in groups, be led by a course leader or discuss problems in front of others, all of which made UK course leaders cautious.

Many writers consider that the best way of minimising threats to integrity is to implement effective process monitoring systems. Hollin suggests three possible sources: outside observers; practitioner report; and offender report. Outside observers can bring greater objectivity to the task, especially when judging the quality of intervention. McIvor (1995) recommends that process monitoring be undertaken by practitioners (through written reports) on the grounds of convenience, although there is some evidence from meta-analyses (e.g. Lipsey, 1992), that outcome evaluations which use practitioner/offender reports produce significantly higher effect sizes, indicating a potential source of bias. Careful process evaluations can not only ensure that programmes are implemented as originally intended but also help to discover which elements of programmes are successful: *"If the intervention process is clearly structured and analysed it is also possible to work out, for example, the central elements of multi modal approaches"* (Losel, 1993 pp 430–431). This would obviously be advantageous in clarifying the contribution of cognitive-behavioural work to the success of programmes which use this type of approach in combination with others, such as life skills or social skills.

Finally, the research literature emphasises that process evaluations should not be confined to treatment groups, as unlike in medical trials where control groups receive 'nothing', offenders are subject to interventions during the course of a prison sentence or probation order which may well impact upon future offending behaviour.

Staff and management issues

Factors such as the level of staff motivation, training, the social climate of an institution, and its relationship with partnership agencies can all affect programme effectiveness (Losel, 1993; Mair, 1995; Hollin, 1993). Empirical data on how and why this occurs is limited but certain factors have been identified and potential solutions have been offered.

Roberts (1995) suggests that in any criminal justice setting a clear organisational plan is required to show the range of provision available to offenders and the practitioners or agencies best able to provide it. Roberts theorises a pyramid structure with 'individual offender focus' at the apex and 'community focus' at the base: a movement down the pyramid increases the likelihood that staff from other community agencies will be involved in providing work to offenders, as the focus of a particular programme becomes less related to offending behaviour. At the apex, Roberts places courses aimed at improving reasoning/cognitive abilities and skills, which may be managed and taught by trained probation officers via individual or group work. Below, are courses with a 'direct offending focus' such as sex offending, and further down are courses aimed at rectifying problems which Roberts sees as having an 'indirect/associated focus' such as alcohol and drug abuse, assertiveness training and handling violence or aggression. At the base of the pyramid, provision such as TEC or educational courses, will be delivered by external agencies such as further education colleges, possibly supported by the probation service or other statutory agencies. Roberts argues that organisational plans of this type can be drawn up by middle management and can be used to identify gaps in service provision, including an absence of cognitive-behavioural work.

Burnett's (1996) research suggests that, although probation officers are increasingly adopting cognitive-behavioural approaches (29% of practitioners identified with this approach), some were notably vague about the methods and theoretical underpinnings of their work. Two - thirds of senior probation officers described officers as being essentially eclectic, both in their use of methods and theories of criminal behaviour. Our own survey of probation programmes confirmed that staff do not distinguish between cognitive skills and cognitive-behavioural methods in describing programmes which include a cognitive component. These findings are, perhaps, unsurprising given the lack of consensus noted earlier in this paper with regard to the definition and classification of cognitive and cognitive-behavioural interventions. The findings may also reflect the focus of existing probation officer training upon a social work model of offending behaviour, and the lack of emphasis upon relevent psychological theory and practice.

Other studies indicate, however, that there may be some resistance towards an approach which attributes the behaviour of offenders to individual personality and circumstances. In his study of 'Reasoning and Rehabilitation' programmes in the UK McGuire (1995a), for example, found some opposition from staff on the grounds that cognitive-behavioural programmes were seen as incompatible with explanations of criminal behaviour that stress environmental factors such as social deprivation, unemployment etc. If such opposition is widespread then the effectiveness of programmes could be diminished (Ross and Ross, 1995). As Ross and Ross, (1995) point out, however, there is no inherent conflict between these explanations, as poor education and an impoverished social and family environment are often a cause of cognitive impairment and consequent delinquent behaviour. Shifting the focus of work with offenders towards their patterns of thinking and relating to others may, nevertheless, require more than simply teaching probation officers new skills and implementing improved organisational structures for assessing need and delivering suitable programmes. The research evidence suggests that probation officers will be more receptive towards an approach which explicitly addresses social and environmental factors associated with criminal behaviour as well as offenders' anti-social attitudes and cognitive deficits.

Conclusion

The findings from several literature reviews and meta-analytic studies of rehabilitative programmes carried out with offenders have challenged the view that 'nothing works'. Although these reviews do not identify particular programmes or techniques associated with large reductions in offending across the broad range of offenders, there is evidence of moderate reductions with selected groups of offenders. A question of central concern to the probation service in England and Wales is whether the incorporation of the messages from this literature can increase the effectiveness of the service in reducing reoffending.

One such message, consistently reported in the meta-analytic studies in the field of offender rehabilitation, is that the type of approach used to address offending behaviour matters. Programmes which draw upon cognitive skills and behavioural methods are reported as achieving higher levels of effectiveness than those which employ group or individual counselling and favour traditional non-directive therapy. The use of cognitive-behavioural methods in a multi modal programme which includes life skills and social skills training shows the most positive results with both juvenile and adult offenders. This combination of components and techniques has also shown some success when targetted on particular groups of offenders–notably, sex offenders and violent offenders–although in most such studies the assessment of effectiveness is confined to clinical outcomes.

Certain important caveats surround these seemingly promising findings. The first is that the research literature does not demonstrate that cognitive-behavioural approaches, or indeed, any other type of approach, routinely produce major reductions in reoffending among a mixed population of offenders. Meta-analytic studies such as that undertaken by Lipsey report a very large distribution in the effects of programmes on recidivism. Among mixed populations of offenders, programmes might achieve a reduction in recidivism of some 10–15 per cent against an 'untreated' comparison group and larger differences have been reported where programmes have been targetted on high risk offenders and upon criminogenic needs. But as Palmer (1994) concluded, it is not possible to identify any all-purpose methods of forms of intervention as being reliably and consistently better than standard, or traditional programmes with offenders. This is, perhaps, unsurprising if it is accepted that the way in which a programme is delivered needs to be adapted to the problems and learning styles of offenders, albeit without undermining programme integrity. Moreover, as Blackburn (1995, p363) has observed, *"the functional relationship of cognitive deficits to criminal behaviour remains unclear"*.

A related difficulty is that many of the original research studies synthesised in meta-analytic reviews lack theoretically grounded explanations as to why certain programme components and styles of delivery are likely to be more or less successful with different types of offender. Typically, the reports mention only in general terms the theoretical 'school' on which the treatment was based. As Pawson and Tilly (1992) have observed in their critique of evaluative studies in the fields of correction and crime prevention, the use of experimental designs, which involve random allocation or matching actually restrict the scope for identifying for whom and why particular types of intervention work. Overall positive effect sizes are indicative of positive change, but they do not elucidate the mechanisms which may explain why some types of offender benefit more than others from a particular type of approach. Thus, for example, there remains considerable uncertainty about precisely what sorts of cognitive and behavioural techniques work best, under what conditions (such as treatment intensity) and types of setting and with whom. Hence, Losel has cautioned that:

> *"One should be careful about sweeping labels such as 'cognitive-behavioural' or 'appropriate' programs as sign posts for a royal path to success...More well-controlled and replicated evaluations of specific programs are necessary"* (Losel (1995) quoted in Hollin and Palmer, 1995).

Notwithstanding these caveats, Losel and others who have reviewed the evidence from large scale meta-analyses of offender programmes are in broad agreement that certain features are associated with the more successful types of intervention with offenders and that there are some clear trends which form a guide for future work with offenders and related evaluation. Although there is some question as to whether the evidence regarding key success factors is as strong as has been widely claimed, the indication from the few better designed studies which have examined both programme content and manner of delivery, is that programmes are unlikely to achieve their objectives unless they adhere to good practice principles drawn from the 'what works' literature. These include: targeting on factors which have contributed to the offending behaviour of those taking part; adopting methods to which those participating are responsive (typically structured, active participation and concrete problem solving); matching degree of intervention to likely future risk of offending; and programme integrity. To ensure the latter, those managing and running the programme must understand and accept its objectives and adhere to the agreed methods.

The inconclusive findings of the literature reviews and meta-analyses summarised in this report point to the need in this country for rigorous evaluation of existing and future programmes which incorporate cognitive-behavioural methods and the principles of effective assessment and delivery. Well-designed and carefully evaluated small-scale studies can, of course, be informative but are no substitute for larger scale studies which are able to achieve higher standards with regard to sampling and design and have the potential for replication with a different sample in a different setting. Such studies should make use of [multivariate] statistical techniques in order to begin to distinguish which programme features and other factors (including the good practice principles, offence and offender characteristics) are most strongly associated with successful programmes. Programmes included in an evaluation should make explicit the underlying theory as to how they are expected to effect change, having regard to existing knowledge of the diverse causes of crime. Evaluations must include measurement of change in the targetted attitudes, behaviour or skills as well as in reconviction rates. More information is needed about the types of offender who are responsive to interventions which use cognitive-behavioural approaches and about the intensity of work needed to bring about a sustained effect. Although the literature suggests that the intensity of work with offenders should be based on the level of risk posed by the offender there is still much to be learnt about the optimum level of intervention for different levels of risk. Similarly, much more research is needed into the way in which programme components and techniques can be matched to offenders needs in such a way as to achieve a long term reduction in reoffending. While the results for 'bought-in' programmes such as Reasoning and Rehabilitation developed in Canada by Ross and Fabiano, are promising, questions remain as to how to adapt such programmes to a UK setting and to maintain the positive effects achieved over a longer period.

Part II:
The influence of cognitive approaches: a survey of probation programmes.

Carol Hedderman and Darren Sugg

The influence of cognitive approaches: a survey of probation programmes

Introduction

In February 1996 the Offenders and Corrections Unit of the Home Office sent out a questionnaire to all probation areas asking for information about the extent to which the programmes they operated, or had access to, made use of cognitive skills training. Cognitive skills was defined for the purposes of this survey as an approach which attempted to reduce reoffending by teaching offenders to analyse and modify their thinking.

This paper describes the results of the survey. The next section describes how many areas have such programmes; the nature and number of programmes in operation; and why they were set up. This is followed by information on the type and number of offenders for whom these programmes cater; how offenders are selected; and whether participation is voluntary or compulsory. The third section focuses on who manages the programmes and the level and sources of training those running the programmes receive. The use of partnerships is also discussed. The extent and quality of programme monitoring and evaluation is then considered together with any evidence respondents were able to provide on the efficacy of the programmes they described and how much they cost. The report concludes with a discussion of the general picture the survey provides of the use of cognitive techniques by the Probation Service in the mid-1990s.

The number and nature of cognitive skills programmes

Thirty - nine areas provided information on 191 programmes and four areas said they did not run programmes with a cognitive skills component-a response rate of 78 per cent. Of the remaining 12 areas, two had amalgamated and were not in a position to provide information and seven were in the process of restructuring their entire system for providing programmes and were reluctant to take part in the survey. Only three areas failed to reply at all to the survey despite being sent a further two reminders.

Of the 39 areas which responded to the survey and ran programmes with a cognitive skills component, two-thirds ran between five and ten programmes, with only six running a single programme. Of the 191 programmes on which details were provided, 118 (62%) were available across each probation area compared with 23 (12%) which only covered some parts of a service. Information on geographic coverage was not available on the other 50 schemes.

As noted in the review of research, cognitive-behavioural approaches encompass a wide range of over-lapping techniques which appear under various labels in the literature. For example, interpersonal skills training, which may include role-play and modelling is categorised in one study as 'cognitive-behavioural' in another as 'cognitive' and in another as 'life-skills'. As Palmer (1994) notes, some category boundaries are still somewhat fluid in this relatively new research area. Thus, while our request for information was carefully framed to elicit information about cognitive skills work, it was clear from the responses that most areas used the terms "cognitive skills" and "cognitive-behavioural" interchangeably. This means that we cannot always accurately distinguish between programmes which include an element of cognitive skills training and those which also used behavioural techniques, unless replies referred to specific programmes such as the Reasoning and Rehabilitation (R % R) programme developed by Ross et al. (1989).

As the first two rows of Table 2.1 shows, general programmes were more popular than those which focused on a particular form of offending. Self control/anger management programmes including those based on the Reasoning and Rehabilitation approach were most heavily used, followed by those based on McGuire and Priestley's offending behaviour programme. Among the programmes which targeted particular offences, those for treating sex offenders and for tackling poor driving behaviour were the most common.

The 'other' group in Table 2.1 comprises those programmes which we were unable to group thematically either because they were unique or because we received too little information about them. For example, one area ran what it called a 'citizenship' programme and another ran something called 'offending is not the only choice'. Similarly, too little information on a number of Probation Centre programmes was received to classify them according to their objectives.

Table 2.1 The sorts of programmes available

Programme Type	No. of programmes	No. of areas
Self-control (inc R and R)	34	24
Offending behaviour	19	14
Sex offending	33	26
Substance abuse	23	18
Motoring	37	22
Domestic violence	7	7
Burglary/theft	2	2
Probation Centre programmes	15	13
For women offenders	7	7
Other	14	10
Total	191	39

The research literature is unclear about precisely which cognitive skills and cognitive-behavioural techniques are the most effective and how far they should be combined with other methods, although practitioners are encouraged to adopt a "multimodal" approach. In the survey, 15 programmes (8%) were based solely on cognitive skills or cognitive-behavioural techniques and a further 12 per cent of programmes were mainly based on these approaches. In total 57 per cent of programmes used cognitive skills for more than half their duration. There were some noteworthy differences between types of programmes, however, those focusing on self-control and sex offending programmes made the heaviest use of cognitive skills training whereas this was usually only one component of substance abuse and driving behaviour courses.

Over 60 per cent of programmes used cognitive skills training to address problems to do with self-control. A similar proportion used it in promoting victim awareness/empathy. Just over half (53%) employed cognitive techniques in promoting relapse prevention and 56 per cent used it in tackling denial. Cognitive skills training was also used for teaching critical reasoning (51%); emotional control (47 per cent); to encourage offenders to be less egocentric (43%); and to promote an appreciation of the difference between abstract and concrete thinking (42 per cent).

Nearly two-thirds of programmes used groupwork exclusively and a third combined this with one-to-one working. Only four programmes relied solely on the latter. As Table 2.2 shows, sex offender programmes were the most intensive and lasted the longest. On average, such programmes also seemed to be nearly one and a half times as long than those reported on by Beckett et al. (1994) when the average length of probation-run programmes for sex offenders was around 60 hours.

Table 2.2 Duration of programmes

Programme Type	Average no. of hours per programme		Duration in weeks	
	Group	Individual	Group	Individual
Offending behaviour	32	4	7	3.5
Self-control	33	8	7	8
Sex offending	88	29	33	22
Substance misuse	16	7	6	5
Motoring	24	9	8	8
All other	50	31	10	10
No information	48			
Total N = 191	41	20	12	11

Programmes which use cognitive skills training are a comparatively new development in most probation areas. Half of the programmes (N=98) had been running for less than five years, and a further quarter had been running for less than a year. Programmes aimed at improving self-control and anger management were particularly likely to be a recent development, with more than eight out of 10 of these being set up within the last five years. Only 11 programmes in total had been running for more than 10 years. However, 134 programmes (in 35 areas) were said to have grown out of previous work with offenders in the respondent's own areas.

The decision to set up cognitive-behavioural programmes was often influenced by a combination of factors, but more than half (53%) of respondents cited successful results in other probation areas. Forty - four per cent of programmes had been initiated because the approach had been championed by a member of staff; and a third of programmes–mainly those dealing with sex offenders or developing self-control–had been influenced by research from abroad.

Only 35 programmes in 17 areas were bought-in, 14 of which focused on self-control/anger management training. The remainder were offending behaviour (four), sex offending, substance abuse and driving (three each), and eight other individual programmes.

Table 2.3 The integrity of bought-in programmes

Programme Type	Duration:		Intensity:	
	Unchanged	Adapted	Unchanged	Adapted
Offending behaviour	3	1	3	1
Self-control (inc R and R)	4	10	5	9
Sex offending	1	2	-	3
Substance misuse	-	3	-	3
Motoring	-	3	-	3
All other	3	5	3	5
All programmes	11	24	11	24

As Table 2.3 shows, the intensity and duration of bought-in programmes were more often altered than not. We did not collect many details about the nature of such changes, but the fact that they occurred (even on highly structured programmes such as "Reasoning and Rehabilitation") suggests that programme integrity is not being maintained.

Selection criteria and take-up rates

Areas were asked to provide information on the sorts of offenders who were targetted by programmes. They revealed that most programmes were designed for adult (over 21) offenders, although many would accept young offenders. One area had a substance abuse programme specifically for young offenders and two motoring programmes were also run separately for offenders aged 17 to 21. On the whole motoring and substance abuse programmes tended to exclude violent offenders whereas (unsurprisingly) self-control programmes targetted them.

Information on the number of men and women currently on programmes was only available for 123 programmes (64%). At the time of the survey seven were programmes run specifically for women, with an average of seven participants. A further 25 programmes accepted women offenders; in these programmes the average male to female ratio was 10:1. Aside from driving behaviour courses, which averaged 16 males/programme, the average number attending other types of programmes was about a dozen.

The survey returns indicate a lack of systematic monitoring of programme use by ethnic group. Only 99 programmes said that ethnic monitoring statistics were collected, of which 58 were able to give precise ethnic breakdown figures for those attending at the time of the survey (February 1996). These programmes were serving 602 white, 40 black and 10 Asian offenders. All those from ethnic minorities were on 22 of the 58 programmes.

We were sent information on only one programme specifically for an ethnic group (Offending behaviour for black offenders run by the West Midlands Probation Service). Unfortunately, no ethnic breakdown figures were provided for this programme, although we were told that this information was collected.

Table 2.4 attending programmes as a requirement of an order*

Programme type	Voluntary only	Additional requirement only	Mixed	Accepts parolees	Total
Offending behaviour	1	4	3	4	11
Self-control	3	8	8	8	21
Sex offending	1	4	12	18	25
Substance abuse	-	11	4	2	15
Motoring	1	18	8	2	28
All other	–	22	11	5	35
Total	6	67	46	39	135

*Rows do not total because parolees could attend separate or mixed groups

Information on the extent to which attendance on a programme was a condition of an order or was voluntary was provided for 135 programmes. As Table 2.4 shows, most programmes were primarily run for those attending as a condition of a court order, but few excluded participation by other offenders attending on a voluntary basis. Perhaps the most noteworthy aspects of Table 2.4 are that so many of the programmes for sex offenders mixed those on additional requirements and those attending voluntarily; and so many accepted offenders on parole. While mixing offenders in this way may be an efficient use of resources, it seems likely that those whose attendance was made compulsory are more serious offenders requiring more intensive treatment. On the other hand, respondents comments suggest that simply basing allocation decisions on seriousness of offence would not necessarily target those most in need:

> Handling Conflict course, Lancashire: *"for adults who have difficulty coping with provocative or anger producing incidents, and whose offending has resulted from a loss of control".*

> Training for Responsible Alternatives to crime, Devon: probation order, suitable for those with a history of persistent property offending, or *"those with a mixture of previous convictions whose offences appear to be ill-conceived, impulsive attempts to solve problems through crime".*

Management, training and staffing

As McGuire (1996) stresses, a cognitive-behavioural approach does not necessarily attribute the causes of criminal behaviour solely to the individual or psychological factors. It also takes into account the social and environmental factors which may influence individual development. That said, cognitive skills training and cognitive-behavioural work is derived from psychological theory and practice, whereas traditionally one-to-one probation work is founded on a sociological understanding of the causes of offending and how to reduce reoffending. At first sight, therefore, probation staff may find it difficult to accept the validity of cognitive skills techniques and may (unintentionally) undermine the integrity of cognitive skills and cognitive-behavioural programmes. To avoid this it is clearly important that programmes are either adequately staffed by probation officers who are properly trained in the theories and concepts which underpin cognitive-behaviourism and in the techniques they are being asked to employ; or that programmes are run by or with specialists through partnership arrangements. It is also important that programmes are well and closely managed.

In 18 of the 39 areas which responded to the survey, one officer had overall responsibility for the management of cognitive-behavioural programmes, although in only one case was this an ACPO. In 16 areas this function was carried out by senior probation officers and in one area (with only one programme) responsibility rested with a probation officer.

Staffing figures were received for 141 programmes in 32 areas. These showed that each programme was run by an average of four probation staff. Three-quarters of those staffing programmes were probation officers, eight per cent were senior probation officers, and the remainder were probation service officers. Only a third of the staff working on programmes did so full-time.

While it is encouraging to note from Table 2.5 that three-quarters of probation staff involved in delivering cognitive skills programmes receive some form of training, 24 per cent did not. Those working on sex offender and anger management programmes were most likely to have received training and were most likely to have been trained by psychologists. However, for other types of programmes most training was carried out by more experienced colleagues or "other external specialists". This group included staff from drug or alcohol agencies or the NSPCC, but also included ex-probation officers.

From comments made by a number of respondents it was clear that the consequences of inadequate training were recognised and felt:

An area running eight programmes found difficulties in *"encouraging officers to give up some of their autonomy both in relation to referrals and breach"* and *"encouraging officers to take-on 'what works' principles"*.

Another respondent commented *"we perceive a need for broader training, perhaps on a national or regional level, with a much more thorough theoretical base to ensure practitioners really understand the concepts and maintain integrity...whilst adapting for a range of offender needs"*.

Table 2.5 Source of training

	No. of programmes	No. of areas
Training provided by:		
Psychologists	28	14
Other external experts	78	30
Experienced colleagues only	37	15
No details	11	4
	143 (74%)	32
No training	45 (24%)	13
No information	3 (2%)	1
Total	191 (100%)	39.00

Table 2.6 shows the range of staff from other agencies who are involved in delivering cognitive skills programmes with probation staff. Around half of the sex offending and substance misuse programmes which responded used outside helpers such as social workers, psychologists and, in the case of the latter, workers from organisations specialising in dealing with substance abuse. Only three programmes used previous offenders, two of which were driving programmes. Police officers were most likely to be involved in driving programmes and prison staff were usually involved in programmes which accepted offenders on parole. Community theatre or arts groups were used across the full range of programmes.

Table 2.6 The involvement of other staff in programme delivery

Agency	No. of programmes	No. of areas
Drug/alcohol workers	18 (9%)	12
Community theatre/arts	16 (8%)	10
Psychologists	15 (8%)	11
NHS	5 (3%)	3
Social services	7 (4%)	7
Previous offenders	3 (2%)	3
NSPCC/child protection org.	6 (3%)	5
Specialist cognitive centres	1 (0.5%)	1
Police	14 (7%)	9
Prison	5 (3%)	2
Domestic violence workers	1 (0.5%)	1
Other	11 (6%)	8
No involvement of other agency	105 (55%)	31*
Total	191**	39

* 31 areas ran at least one programme with no involvement from other agencies
** Some programmes involved staff from more than one agency

While the involvement of outside experts may, in part, compensate for probation officers' lack of training, it is noteworthy that programmes with well-trained staff tended to be the ones which most often involved outside specialists (and of course not all of the staff from other agencies will themselves be trained in cognitive techniques).

Partnerships

Twenty - nine of the 39 areas made use of partnership arrangements in just under half (89) of the 191 programmes they ran. Partnership arrangements were most common with Social Services (25 programmes), community theatre or art groups (23 programmes), and substance misuse agencies or the NHS (21 programmes). Other, less common, partnerships were with the NSPCC or other children protection agencies, specialist cognitive centres and domestic violence workers. The ten areas which did not use partnerships did not appear to be unusual in any way, running 47 programmes (13 self-control programmes, eight driving programmes, six offending behaviour, six sex offending programmes, four substance abuse and 10 'other').

Table 2.7 Types of programmes and partnership arrangements

Programme type	No. of programmes	No. run in partnership	More than one partner
Self-control (R and R)	36	13	2
Offending behaviour	19	5	2
Sex offending	33	20	6
Substance misuse	23	14	4
Driving behaviour	35	21	6
Other	45	16	3
Total	191	89 (47%)	23

The returns show that certain types of programmes are more likely to be run in partnership than others (Table 2.7). Sixty per cent of sex offender, driving behaviour and substance misuse programmes are run in partnership with external agencies, compared with half of the drug and alcohol programmes and just over a third of self-control and offending behaviour courses. Social Services were almost invariably one of the partners where more than one partner was involved in running a programme.

Overall the survey suggests that it is the type of provision that a service wishes to provide (e.g. sex offender programmes, driving behaviour) that dictates whether and what type of partnership agencies are used, although a small number of areas are more orientated towards partnership than others.

Five areas reported having problems with partnership agencies. Although some of these were financial, others were said to stem from the differences in probation and partners approaches and attitudes. For example, in one area which uses partnership agencies quite extensively there were problems in *"inducting 'partners' into our ethics and culture"*.

Monitoring, evaluation and costs

Only five areas admitted that they did not monitor the impact of the programmes they ran, although three of these said that they did have plans to do so. Most other areas (n=18) said that they collected basic monitoring information, such as referral, completion and compliance rates, but only six areas provided any information to support this. Given how few areas were able to provide information on the numbers attending programmes, such claims should be treated with a degree of caution. Fifteen areas said that success was measured by seeking offenders' views. Ten areas claimed to measure attitudinal change, mainly using CRIME-PICS. In twelve areas offenders' views were collected in addition to collecting basic monitoring data, but in two areas it appeared to be an alternative. Nine areas said they sought feedback from staff as a measure of success but several stretched this to include weekly management meetings. Only five areas claimed they either collect reconviction information or intend to do so.

Six areas provided examples of programme evaluations produced by in-house staff. One area provided an interim report from an independent researcher and one provided a copy of a research proposal which the area was committed to supporting.

Of the six internal reports we received from areas: one relied heavily on offender feedback. Unfortunately, the results it contains are unreliable because it asked leading (Likert) questions which encouraged offenders to respond positively (e.g. they were asked how far they agreed with statements such as "I enjoyed the programme" or "I feel I was treated with respect", rather than more neutral statements like "how much did you enjoy the programme?" or "how far did you feel you were treated with respect?"). Another made oversimplistic comparisons between the impact of prison and probation without taking differences in offending into account. It was also based on an extremely small sample (n=21) and comparison group (n=19). Despite this, the author felt able to claim that "offenders completing the probation centre programme were 32 per cent less likely to be reconvicted over a two year period".

The four remaining areas had clearly attempted to carry out thorough examinations of their programmes, combining data from different sources in an effort to present a rounded picture. However, all but one of these evaluations were bedevilled by small numbers and a lack of data on comparison groups.

Only nine areas claimed to have (18) programmes which were being or had been independently evaluated. The one (interim) external report we received refers to plans to use a range of methods–attitudinal questionnaire, group observation, interviews with offenders and staff, and a reconviction study–but only describes basic monitoring information (because it is at an early stage).

The responses to Probation Circular 42/96 showed that very few probation areas were able to provide basic information on the costs of additional requirement programmes. This survey presents a similarly depressing picture. Only 12 areas were able to provide any specific information on costs. Nine provided the overall amount spent on an individual programme or set of programmes, but these varied according to whether staff costs were included. Partly because of this figures ranged from £61,000 per annum to £300,000. Two areas provided a cost per offender and one area (West Yorkshire) was able to provide an hourly breakdown for each programme.

Conclusion

Taken as a whole the survey results reveal that since the late 1980s a majority of probation areas have developed or bought programmes with a cognitive skills or cognitive-behavioural dimension. Two - thirds of the areas which ran such programmes were running between five and ten of them. The limited information provided on costs shows that such programmes do not come cheap, yet areas appear to have spent remarkably little time or effort on examining whether such programmes work. In most areas it seems that they do not even know how many people attend, who drops out and why, and who succeeds and why. While offender and staff feedback can be useful ways of examining how user-friendly such programmes are, they are a poor source of data on overall effectiveness in modifying patterns of thinking and reducing reoffending.

The survey also suggests that while the probation service has picked up on the message that "something works" and recognise that "cognitive skills" and "cognitive-behaviourism" are central to this, they have not committed themselves fully to "what works" principles. In particular, this survey shows a lack of commitment to programme integrity. This is apparent in the fact that the duration and intensity of programmes is commonly altered; and from the fact that staff training is limited or even non-existent.

Programmes also seem to function without reference to risk and needs principles. Mixing offenders on parole with others subject to additional requirements and those attending voluntarily may keep programme numbers high, but is unlikely to achieve programmes which are well matched to the levels of risk, and criminogenic needs, of the offenders who attend. While sex offender programmes tend to be (comparatively) well-organised, run by well-trained staff, and able to draw on outside expertise, they too are rarely restricted to serious offenders.

Perhaps the most encouraging aspect of our findings was that respondents were far from complacent about the way programmes were operating. The frankness of their replies and the use they made of open-ended questions shows that many of those responsible for running the programmes on a day-to-day basis would welcome more training, more advice and better evaluations. They believe their programmes work, but they cannot prove it and they know that many could work even better. One obvious step which could be made would be for a more strategic approach to setting up and running programmes at senior levels–perhaps with programmes being run initially on a pilot basis and properly evaluated before being delivered on a larger scale. Another improvement might be to create a standard set of evaluation measures (which areas could add to but not amend) which would ensure that similar programmes were being compared fairly. It could also enable the results of several small-scale evaluations to be combined, so that sample-sizes were great enough to test for statistical significance, without resorting to less reliable techniques such as meta-analysis.

References

Allsop, B. and Saunders, S. (1989) *Relapse and alcohol problems.* In M. Gossop (Ed), Relapse and Addictive Behaviour. London: Tavistock/Routledge.

Andrews, D.A. (1982). *The Level of Supervision Inventory (LSI): The first follow-up.* Toronto: Ontario Ministry of Correctional Services.

Andrews, D.A. and Bonta, J. (1995). *LSI-R: the level of service inventory-revised.* Toronto: Multi-Health Systems.

Andrews, D.A., Zinger, I., Hoge, R.D, Bonta, J., Gendreau, P. and Cullen, F.T. (1990). *"Does correctional treatment work? A clinically relevant and psychologically informed meta-analysis".* Criminology, 28, 369-404.

Andrews, D.A., Zinger, I., Hoge, R.D., Bonta. J., Gendreau, P. and Cullen, F.T. (1990a) *"A Human Science Approach or more punishment and pessimism: A rejoinder to Lab and Whitehead".* Criminology, 28, 419-429.

Antonowicz, D. and Ross, R. R. (1994). *"Essential components of successful rehabilitation programs for offenders".* International Journal of Offender Therapy and Comparative Criminology, 38, 97-104.

Aubrey, R. and Hough, M. (1997) *"Assessing Offenders' Needs" Assessment Scales for the Probation Service.* Home Office Research Study No 166, London: Home Office.

Ausubel, D. (1958). *Theories and problems of child development.* New York: Grune and Stratton.

Barker, M. and Morgan, R. (1993). *Sex offenders: a framework for the evaluation of community-based treatment.* London: Home Office

Beckett, R., Beech, A., Fisher, D. and Fordham, A S. (1994). *Community-based treatment for sex offenders: an evaluation of seven treatment programmes.* London: Home Office.

Blackburn, R. (1995). *The Psychology of Criminal Conduct: Theory, Research and Practice.* Chichester: Wiley.

Borduin, C.M., Mann, B.J., Cone, L.T., Henggeler, S.W., Fucci, B.R., Blaske., D.M. and Williams, R.A. (1995) *"Multisystemic Treatment of Serious Juvenile Offenders: Long-Term Prevention of Criminality and Violence".* Journal of Consulting and Clinical Psychology. Vol. 63. No. 4, 569-578.

Brown, K. and Howells, K. (1996). *"Violent Offenders".* In: Hollin, C (Ed) Working with Offenders: Psychological Practice in Offender Rehabilitation. Chichester: Wiley

Burnett, R. (1996). *Fitting supervision to offenders: assessment and allocation decisions in the Probation Service.* Home Office Research Study No 153. London: Home Office.

Cooke, David. J. (1996) *"Psychopathy Across Cultures".* In: Forth, A.E., Newman, J. and Hare, R.D. Information Perspectives on Psychopathy. British Psychology Society: Leicester.

Dobash, R. Dobash, R., Cavanagh, K. and Lewis, J. (1996). *Research evaluation of programmes for violent men.* Edinburgh: Scottish Office.

Epps, K. (1996). *"Sex Offenders".* In: Hollin, C (Ed) Working with Offenders: Psychological Practice in Offender Rehabilitation. Chichester: Wiley.

Farrington, D. (1996). *"Criminological Psychology: individual and family factors in the explanation and prevention of offending".* In: Hollin, C (Ed) Working with Offenders: Psychological Practice in Offender Rehabilitation. Chichester: Wiley.

Feindler, E.L. and Ecton, R.B. (1986). *Adolescent Anger Control: Cognitive-behavioral techniques.* New York: Pergamon.

Furby, L., Weinrott, M.R. and Blackshaw, L. (1989). *Sex Offender recidivism: a review.* Psychological Bulletin, 105, 3-30.

Gendreau, P. and Ross, R.R. (1979). *"Effective correctional treatment: Bibliotherapy for cynics".* Crime and Delinquency, 25, 463-489.

Gendreau, P. and Andrews, D.A. (1990). *"Tertiary Prevention: What the Meta-analyses of the Offender Treatment Literature Tell Us About 'What Works'".* Canadian Journal of Criminology. Ontario.

Gendreau, P. (1995) *"Successful Strategies for Implementing Programmes in Community Corrections"* In: Unpublished. Home Office: ACOP & CPC Conference Report.

Glick, B. and Goldstein, A.P. (1987). *Aggression Replacement Training* Champaign, IL: Research Press.

Glick, B., Goldstein, A., Irwin, M.J., Pask-McCartney, C., and Rubama, I. (1989) *Reducing Delinquency: interventions in the community.* New York: Pergamon.

Glueck, S. and Glueck, E. (1950). *Unraveling juvenile delinquency.* New York: Harper and Row.

Hare, R.D. (1980) *A research scale for the assessment of psychopathy in criminal populations.* Personality and Individual difference, 1,111-119.

Hare, R.D. (1991). *The Hare Psychopathy Checklist-revised.* Toronto: Multi-Health Systems.

Hedderman, C. and Sugg, D. *(1996) "Does Treating Sex Offenders Reduce reoffending?"* Research Finding No. 45. London: Home Office.

Hollin, C. R. (1990). *Cognitive-behavioral interventions with Young Offenders.* New York: Pergamon.

Hollin, C.R. (1993). *"Advances in the psychological treatment of delinquent behaviour".* Criminal Behaviour and Mental Health, 3, 142-157.

Hollin, C. R. (1994). *"Designing effective rehabilitation programmes for young offenders".* Psychology, Crime and Law, 1, 193-199.

Hollin, C.R. (1995) *"The Meaning and Implications of 'Programme Integrity'".* In: McGuire. J. (Ed) What Works: Reducing re-offending. Chichester: Wiley.

Hollin, C. R. (1996). *"Young Offenders".* In: Hollin, C (Ed) Working with Offenders: Psychological Practice in Offender Rehabilitation. Chichester: Wiley.

Hollin, C.R and Palmer, E.J. (1995) *Assessing prison regimes: A review to inform the development of outcome measures.* Report for the Prison Service. Birmingham: University of Birmingham. Unpublished.

Hough, M. (1995) *"Drugs Misuse and the Criminal Justice System: a review of the literature"*. Drugs Prevention Initiative, Paper 15. London: Home Office.

Husband, S.D. and Platt, J.J. (1993). *"The cognitive skills component in substance abuse treatment in correctional settings: a brief review"*. Journal of Drug Issues, 23, 31-45.

Izzo, R.J. and Ross, R.R. (1990). *"Meta-analysis of rehabilitation programmes for juvenile delinquents"*. Criminal Justice and Behaviour, 17, 144-167.

Johnson, V.S. (1981). *"Staff drift: A problem of treatment integrity"*. Criminal Justice and Behaviour, 8, 223-232.

Johnson, G. and Hunter, R.M. (1995) *"Evaluation of the specialised drug offender program"*. In: Ross, R.D., and Ross, D.R., (Ed) Thinking Straight: the Reasoning and Rehabilitation program for Delinquency Prevention and Offender Rehabilitation. Air Training and Publications: Ottawa.

Kemshall, H. (1996) *Reviewing risk: a review of research in the assesment and management of risk and dangerousness: implications for policy and practice in the probation service*. London: Home Office.

Klein, N.C., Alexander, J.F. and Parsons, B.V. (1977). *"Impact of family systems intervention on recidivism and sibling delinquency: A model of primary prevention and program evaluation"* Journal of Consulting and Clinical Psychology, 51, 655-660.

Knott, C. (1995). *"The STOP Programme: Reasoning and Rehabilitation in a British Setting"*. In: McGuire, J. (Ed) What Works: Reducing Reoffending. Chichester: Wiley.

Lab, S.P. and Whitehead, J.T. (1990). *"From 'Nothing Works' to 'The appropriate Works': The latest stop on the search for the secular grail"* Criminology, 28, 405-417.

Leeman, L.W., Gibbs, J.C and Fuller, D. *(1993). "Evaluation of a multi-component group treatment programme for juvenile delinquents"*. Aggressive Behaviour, 19, 281-292

Lipsey, M. W. (1992). *"The effect of treatment on juvenile delinquents: results from meta-analysis"*. In: Losel, F., Bliesener, T. and Bender, D. (Eds) Psychology and Law: International Perspectives. Berlin: de Gruyter.

Lipsey, M. W. (1995). *"What do we learn from 400 research studies on the effectiveness of treatment with juvenile delinquents?"*. In: McGuire, J. (Ed) What Works: Reducing Reoffending. Chichester: Wiley.

Lloyd, C., Mair, G. and Hough, M. (1994). *Explaining reconviction rates: a critical analysis.* Home Office Research Study 136. London: HMSO.

Lochman, J.E. (1992). *"Cognitive-behavioural intervention with aggressive boys: three-year follow-up and preventive effects"*. Journal of Consulting and Clinical Psychology, 60, 426-432

Losel, F. (1993). *"The effectiveness of treatment in institutional and community settings"*. Criminal Behaviour and Mental Health, 3, 416-437.

Losel, F. (1995). *"The efficacy of correctional treatment: A review and synthesis of meta-evaluations"*. In: McGuire, J. (Ed) What Works: Reducing Reoffending. Chichester: Wiley.

Losel, F., Koferl, P. and Weber, F. (1987). *Meta-evaluation of Social Therapy.* Stuttgart: Enke.

Mair, G. (1995). *"Evaluating the impact of community penalties"*. University of Chicago Law School Roundtable, vol 2, no 2, 455-474

Mair, G., Lloyd, C., Nee, C. and Sibbitt, R. (1994) *"Intensive Probation in England and Wales: An evaluation"*. Home Office Research Study No. 133. London: HMSO.

Mair, G. and Copas J. (1996) *"Nothing Works and What Works–Meta-Analysis?"* British Journal of Criminology. Unpublished.

Martinson, R. (1974). *"What works? Questions and answers about prison reform"*. Public Interest, 10, 22-54.

Marques, J. (1994). *"Effects of cognitive-behavioural treatment on sex offender recidivism: preliminary results of a longitudinal study"*. Criminal Justice and Behaviour, 21, 28-54.

Marshall, W.L. and Barbaree, H.E. (1990). *Outcome of comprehensive cognitive-behavioral treatment programs.* In: Marshall, W.L, Laws, D.R., and Barbaree, H.E (eds) Handbook of sexual assualt: Issues, Theories, and treatment of the Offender. New York: Plenum.

Marshall, W.L., Ward, T., Johnson, P. and Barbaree, H.E. (1991). *Treatment outcome with sex offenders.* Clinical Psychology Review, 11, 465-485.

Mayer, J.P., Gensheimer, L.K., Davidson II, W.S. and Gottschalk, R. (1986). *"Social learning treatment within juvenile justice: A meta-analysis of impact in the natural environment".* In: Apter, S.J and Goldstein (Eds). Youth Violence: Programs and Prospects. Elmsford: Pergamon Press.

Mayhew. P., Aye Maung, N. and Mirrlees-Black, C. *(1993) "The 1992 British Crime Survey":* Home Office Research Study No. 132, London: HMSO.

McDougall, C., Barnett, R.M, Ashurst, B. and Willis, B. (1987) *"Cognitive control of anger".* In: McGurk, B.J., Thornton, D.M., and Williams, M. (eds) Applying Psychology to imprisonment: Theories and Practice. London: HMSO.

McGuire, J. and Priestley, P. (1995). *"Reviewing 'What Works': Past, Present and Future".* In: McGuire, J. (Ed) What Works: Reducing Reoffending. Chichester: Wiley

McGuire, J., Broomfield D., D., Robinson, C. and Rowson, B. (1995). *"Short-term impact of probation programs: an evaluation study".* International Journal of Offender Therapy and Comparative Criminology, 39, 23-42.

McGuire, J. (1995) (Ed) *"What Works: Reducing Reoffending".* Chichester: Wiley.

McGuire, J. (1995a) *"Community-based Reasoning & Rehabilitation Programs in the UK"* In: Ross, R.D., and Ross, D.R., (Ed) Thinking Straight: the Reasoning and Rehabilitation program for Delinquency Prevention and Offender Rehabilitation. Air Training and Publications: Ottawa.

McGuire, J. (1996) *"Cognitive-Behavioural Approaches": An introductory course on theory and research.* Course Manual: University of Liverpool.

McGuire, J. (1996a). *"Community-based interventions"* In: Hollin, C (Ed) Working with Offenders: Psychological Practice in Offender Rehabilitation. Chichester: Wiley.

McIvor, G. (1995). *"Practitioner evaluation in probation".* In: McGuire, J. (Ed) What Works: Reducing Reoffending. Chichester: Wiley.

McMurran, M. (1996). *"Alcohol, Drugs and Criminal Behaviour"* In: Hollin, C (Ed) Working with Offenders: Psychological Practice in Offender Rehabilitation. Chichester: Wiley.

McMurran, M. and Hollin, C.R. (1993). *Young offenders and alcohol-related crime: A practitioner's guidebook.* Chichester: Wiley.

Novaco, R.W. (1975) *Anger Control: the development and evaluation of an experimental treatment.* Lexington: MA.

Novaco, R.W (1978) *"Anger and Coping with stress".* In: Foreyt, J.P and Rathjen, D.P. Cognitive Behavior Therapy. New York: Plenum.

Palmer, T. (1975). *Martinson revisited.* Journal of Research in Crime and Delinquency, 12, 133-152.

Palmer, T. (1994). *A profile of correctional effectiveness and new directions for research.* Albany: State University of New York.

Panizzon, A.G., Olson-Raymer and Guerra, N. (1991). *Delinquency Prevention: What works/What doesn't.* Sacremento: Office of Criminal Justice Planning.

Pawson, R., and Tilly, N. (1992). *Re-evaluation: rethinking research on corrections and crime.* In: Yearbook of correctional education 1992.

Platt, Jerome, J., Perry, Gerald, M. and Metzger, David. S. (1980). *"An Evaluation of Heroin Addiction Treatment Program within a Correctional Enviroment"* In R.R. Ross and P Gendeau (eds) "Effective Correctional Treatment". Toronto: Butterworths 1980.

Proctor, E. and Flaxington, F. (1996). *Community based interventions with sex offenders organised by the Probation Service.* Association of Chief Officers of Probation.

Raynor, P. and Vanstone, M. (1994). *Straight Thinking on Probation: Third Interim Report.* Bridgend: Mid Glamorgan Probation Service.

Raynor, P. and Vanstone, M. (1996). *"Reasoning and Rehabilitation in Britain: the results of the Straight Thinking on Probation (STOP) programme".* International Journal of Offender Therapy and Comparative Criminology, 40 (4) 272-284.

Redondo et al. (1996) *"Is the Treatment of Offenders Effective in Europe?: The Results of a Meta-Analysis".* Presentation at the 48th Annual Meeting of the American Society of Criminology, Chicago, Illinois. Centre of Legal Studies, Spain.

Roberts, C. (1995). *"Effective practice and service delivery"*. In: McGuire, J. (Ed) What Works: Reducing Reoffending. Chichester: Wiley.

Ross, R.R., Fabiano, E. A., and Ewles, C.D. (1988). *"Reasoning and rehabilitation"*. International Journal of Offender Therapy and Comparative Criminology, 32, 29-35.

Ross, R.R., Fabiano, E.A. and Ross, B. (1989). *Reasoning and rehabilitation: A handbook for teaching cognitive skills.* Ottawa: The Cognitive Centre.

Ross, R.D., and Ross, D.R., eds. (1995) *Thinking Straight: the Reasoning and Rehabilitation program for Delinquency Prevention and Offender Rehabilitation.* Air Training and Publications: Ottawa.

Schlicter, K.J. (1978). *'An Application of Stress Innoculation in the Development of Anger Management Skills in Institutionalised Juvenile Delinquents'.* Dissertation: Abstracts International.

Schlicter, K.J. and Horan, J.J. (1981). *"Effects of stress inoculation on the anger and aggression management skills of institutionalized juvenile delinquents"*. Cognitive Therapy and Research, 5, 359-365.

Schneider, A.L., Erwin, L. and Snyder-Joy, Z. (1996). *"Further exploration of the flight from discretion: the role of risk/need instruments in probation supervision decisions"*. Journal of Criminal Justice, 24, 109-121.

Walters, G. D. (1995). *"The psychological inventory of criminal thinking styles Part 1: Reliability and preliminary data"*. Criminal Justice and Behaviour, 22, 307-325.

Whitehead, J.T. and Lab, S.P. (1989). *'A meta-analysis of juvenile correctional treatment"*. Journal of Research in Crime and Delinquency, 26, 276-295.

Publications

List of research publications

A list of research reports for the last three years is provided below. A **full** list of publications is available on request from the Research and Statistics Directorate Information and Publications Group.

Home Office Research Studies (HORS)

133. **Intensive Probation in England and Wales: an evaluation.** George Mair, Charles Lloyd, Claire Nee and Rae Sibbett. 1994. xiv + 143pp. (0 11 341114 6).

134. **Contacts between Police and Public: findings from the 1992 British Crime Survey.** Wesley G Skogan. 1995. ix + 93pp. (0 11 341115 4).

135. **Policing low-level disorder: Police use of Section 5 of the Public Order Act 1986.** David Brown and Tom Ellis. 1994. ix + 69pp. (0 11 341116 2).

136. **Explaining reconviction rates: A critical analysis.** Charles Lloyd, George Mair and Mike Hough. 1995. xiv + 103pp. (0 11 341117 0).

137. **Case Screening by the Crown Prosecution Service: How and why cases are terminated.** Debbie Crisp and David Moxon. 1995. viii + 66pp. (0 11 341137 5).

138. **Public Interest Case Assessment Schemes.** Debbie Crisp, Claire Whittaker and Jessica Harris. 1995. x + 58pp. (0 11 341139 1).

139. **Policing domestic violence in the 1990s.** Sharon Grace. 1995. x + 74pp. (0 11 341140 5).

140. **Young people, victimisation and the police: British Crime Survey findings on experiences and attitudes of 12 to 15 year olds.** Natalie Aye Maung. 1995. xii + 140pp. (0 11 341150 2).

141. **The Settlement of refugees in Britain.** Jenny Carey-Wood, Karen Duke, Valerie Karn and Tony Marshall. 1995. xii + 133pp. (0 11 341145 6).

142. **Vietnamese Refugees since 1982.** Karen Duke and Tony Marshall. 1995. x + 62pp. (0 11 341147 2).

143. **The Parish Special Constables Scheme.** Peter Southgate, Tom Bucke and Carole Byron. 1995. x + 59pp. (1 85893 458 3).

144. **Measuring the Satisfaction of the Courts with the Probation Service.** Chris May. 1995. x + 76pp. (1 85893 483 4).

145. **Young people and crime.** John Graham and Benjamin Bowling. 1995. xv + 142pp. (1 85893 551 2).

146. **Crime against retail and manufacturing premises: findings from the 1994 Commercial Victimisation Survey.** Catriona Mirrlees-Black and Alec Ross. 1995. xi + 110pp. (1 85893 554 7).

147. **Anxiety about crime: findings from the 1994 British Crime Survey.** Michael Hough. 1995. viii + 92pp. (1 85893 553 9).

148. **The ILPS Methadone Prescribing Project.** Rae Sibbitt. 1996. viii + 69pp. (1 85893 485 0).

149. **To scare straight or educate? The British experience of day visits to prison for young people.** Charles Lloyd. 1996. xi + 60pp. (1 85893 570 9).

150. **Predicting reoffending for Discretionary Conditional Release.** John B Copas, Peter Marshall and Roger Tarling. 1996. vii + 49pp. (1 85893 576 8).

151. **Drug misuse declared: results of the 1994 British Crime Survey.** Malcom Ramsay and Andrew Percy. 1996. xv + 131pp. (1 85893 628 4).

152. **An Evaluation of the Introduction and Operation of the Youth Court.** David O'Mahony and Kevin Haines. 1996. viii + 70pp. (1 85893 579 2).

153. **Fitting supervision to offenders: assessment and allocation decisions in the Probation Service.** Ros Burnett. 1996. xi + 99pp. (1 85893 599 7).

155. **PACE: a review of the literature. The first ten years.** David Brown. 1997. xx + 281pp. (1 85893 603 9).

156. **Automatic Conditional Release: the first two years.** Mike Maguire, Brigitte Perroud and Peter Raynor. 1996. x + 114pp. (1 85893 659 4).

157. **Testing obscenity: an international comparison of laws and controls relating to obscene material.** Sharon Grace. 1996. ix + 46pp. (1 85893 672 1).

158. **Enforcing community sentences: supervisors' perspectives on ensuring compliance and dealing with breach.** Tom Ellis, Carol Hedderman and Ed Mortimer. 1996. x + 81pp. (1 85893 691 8).

160. **Implementing crime prevention schemes in a multi-agency setting: aspects of process in the Safer Cities programme.** Mike Sutton. 1996. x + 53pp. (1 85893 691 8).

161. **Reducing criminality among young people: a sample of relevant programmes in the United Kingdom.** David Utting. 1997. vi + 122pp. (1 85893 744 2).

162   **Imprisoned women and mothers.** Dianne Caddle and Debbie Crisp. 1996. xiii + 74pp. (1 85893 760 4).

163. **Curfew orders with electronic monitoring: an evaluation of the first twelve months of the trials in Greater Manchester, Norfolk and Berkshire, 1995 - 1996.** George Mair and Ed Mortimer. 1996. x + 50pp. (1 85893 765 5).

165. **Enforcing financial penalties.** Claire Whittaker and Alan Mackie. 1997. xii + 58pp. (1 85893 786 8).

166. **Assessing offenders' needs: assessment scales for the probation service.** Rosumund Aubrey and Michael Hough. x + 55pp.(1 85893 799 X).

167. **Offenders on probation.** George Mair and Chris May. 1997. xiv + 95pp. (1 85893 890 2).

168. **Managing courts effectively: The reasons for adjournments in magistrates' courts.** Claire Whittaker, Alan Mackie, Ruth Lewis and Nicola Ponikiewski. 1997. x + 37pp. (1 85893 804 X).

169.   **Addressing the literacy needs of offenders under probation supervision.** Gwynn Davis et al. 1997. xiv + 109pp. (1 85893 889 9).

Nos 159 and 164 not published yet.

Research and Planning Unit Papers (RPUP)

81.   **The welfare needs of unconvicted prisoners.** Diane Caddle and Sheila White. 1994.

82.   **Racially motivated crime: a British Crime Survey analysis.** Natalie Aye Maung and Catriona Mirrlees-Black. 1994.

83.   **Mathematical models for forecasting Passport demand.** Andy Jones and John MacLeod. 1994.

84.   **The theft of firearms.** John Corkery. 1994.

85.   **Equal opportunities and the Fire Service.** Tom Bucke. 1994.

86.   **Drug Education Amongst Teenagers: a 1992 British Crime Survey Analysis.** Lizanne Dowds and Judith Redfern. 1995.

87.   **Group 4 Prisoner Escort Service: a survey of customer satisfaction.** Claire Nee. 1994.

88.   **Special Considerations: Issues for the Management and Organisation of the Volunteer Police.** Catriona Mirrlees-Black and Carole Byron. 1995.

89.   **Self-reported drug misuse in England and Wales: findings from the 1992 British Crime Survey.** Joy Mott and Catriona Mirrlees-Black. 1995.

90.   **Improving bail decisions: the bail process project, phase 1.** John Burrows, Paul Henderson and Patricia Morgan. 1995.

91.   **Practitioners' views of the Criminal Justice Act: a survey of criminal justice agencies.** George Mair and Chris May. 1995.

92.   **Obscene, threatening and other troublesome telephone calls to women in England and Wales: 1982-1992.** Wendy Buck, Michael Chatterton and Ken Pease. 1995.

93. **A survey of the prisoner escort and custody service provided by Group 4 and by Securicor Custodial Services.** Diane Caddle. 1995.

Research Findings

8. **Findings from the International Crime Survey.** Pat Mayhew. 1994.

9 **Fear of Crime: Findings from the 1992 British Crime Survey.** Catriona Mirrlees-Black and Natalie Aye Maung. 1994.

10. **Does the Criminal Justice system treat men and women differently?** Carol Hedderman and Mike Hough. 1994.

11. **Participation in Neighbourhood Watch: Findings from the 1992 British Crime Survey.** Lizanne Dowds and Pat Mayhew. 1994.

12. **Explaining Reconviction Rates: A Critical Analysis.** Charles Lloyd, George Mair and Mike Hough. 1995.

13. **Equal opportunities and the Fire Service.** Tom Bucke. 1994.

14. **Trends in Crime: Findings from the 1994 British Crime Survey.** Pat Mayhew, Catriona Mirrlees-Black and Natalie Aye Maung. 1994.

15. **Intensive Probation in England and Wales: an evaluation**. George Mair, Charles Lloyd, Claire Nee and Rae Sibbitt. 1995.

16. **The settlement of refugees in Britain**. Jenny Carey-Wood, Karen Duke, Valerie Karn and Tony Marshall. 1995.

17. **Young people, victimisation and the police: British Crime Survey findings on experiences and attitudes of 12- to 15-year-olds.** Natalie Aye Maung. 1995.

18. **Vietnamese Refugees since 1982.** Karen Duke and Tony Marshall. 1995.

19. **Supervision of Restricted Patients in the Community.** Suzanne Dell and Adrian Grounds. 1995.

20. **Videotaping children's evidence: an evaluation.** Graham Davies, Clare Wilson, Rebecca Mitchell and John Milsom. 1995.

21. **The mentally disordered and the police.** Graham Robertson, Richard Pearson and Robert Gibb. 1995.

22. **Preparing records of taped interviews.** Andrew Hooke and Jim Knox. 1995.

23. **Obscene, threatening and other troublesome telephone calls to women: Findings from the British Crime Survey.** Wendy Buck, Michael Chatterton and Ken Pease. 1995.

24. **Young people and crime.** John Graham and Ben Bowling. 1995.

25. **Anxiety about crime: Findings from the 1994 British Crime Survey.** Michael Hough. 1995.

26. **Crime against retail premises in 1993.** Catriona Mirrlees-Black and Alec Ross. 1995.

27. **Crime against manufacturing premises in 1993.** Catriona Mirrlees-Black and Alec Ross. 1995.

28. **Policing and the public: findings from the 1994 British Crime Survey.** Tom Bucke. 1995.

29. **The Child Witness Pack – An Evaluation.** Joyce Plotnikoff and Richard Woolfson. 1995.

30. **To scare straight or educate? The British experience of day visits to prison for young people.** Charles Lloyd. 1996.

31. **The ADT drug treatment programme at HMP Downview – a preliminary evaluation.** Elaine Player and Carol Martin. 1996.

32. **Wolds remand prison – an evaluation.** Keith Bottomley, Adrian James, Emma Clare and Alison Liebling. 1996.

33. **Drug misuse declared: results of the 1994 British Crime Survey.** Malcolm Ramsay and Andrew Percy. 1996.

34. **Crack cocaine and drugs-crime careers.** Howard Parker and Tim Bottomley. 1996.

35. **Imprisonment for fine default.** David Moxon and Claire Whittaker. 1996.

36. **Fine impositions and enforcement following the Criminal Justice Act 1993.** Elizabeth Charman, Bryan Gibson, Terry Honess and Rod Morgan. 1996.

37. **Victimisation in prisons.** Ian O'Donnell and Kimmett Edgar. 1996.

38   **Mothers in prison.** Dianne Caddle and Debbie Crisp. 1997.

39. **Ethnic minorities, victimisation and racial harassment.** Marian Fitzgerald and Chris Hale. 1996.

40. **Evaluating joint performance management between the police and the Crown Prosecution Service.** Andrew Hooke, Jim Knox and David Portas. 1996.

41. **Public attitudes to drug-related crime.** Sharon Grace. 1996.

42. **Domestic burglary schemes in the safer cities programme.** Paul Ekblom, Ho Law and Mike Sutton. 1996.

43. **Pakistani women's experience of domestic violence in Great Britain.** Salma Choudry. 1996.

44. **Witnesses with learning disabilities.** Andrew Sanders, Jane Creaton, Sophia Bird and Leanne Weber. 1997.

45. **Does treating sex offenders reduce reoffending?** Carol Hedderman and Darren Sugg. 1996.

46. **Re-education programmes for violent men - an evaluation.** Russell Dobash, Rebecca Emerson Dobash, Kate Cavanagh and Ruth Lewis. 1996.

47. **Sentencing without a pre-sentence report.** Nigel Charles, Claire Whittaker and Caroline Ball. 1997.

48   **Magistrates' views of the probation service.** Chris May. 1997.

49. **PACE ten years on: a review of the research.** David Brown. 1997.

53. **A reconviction study of HMP Grendon Therapeutic Community.** Peter Marshall. 1997.

55. **The prevalence of convictions for sexual offending.** Peter Marshall. 1997.

Nos 50 - 52 and 54 not yet published.

Research Bulletin (no longer produced)

The Research Bulletin contains short articles on recent research. Back issues are available on request.

Occasional Papers

Measurement of caseload weightings associated with the Children Act. Richard J. Gadsden and Graham J. Worsdale. 1994. (Available from the RSD Information and Publications Group.)

Managing difficult prisoners: The Lincoln and Hull special units. Professor Keith Bottomley, Professor Norman Jepson, Mr Kenneth Elliott and Dr Jeremy Coid. 1994. (Available from the RSD Information and Publications Group.)

The Nacro diversion initiative for mentally disturbed offenders: an account and an evaluation. Home Office, NACRO and Mental Health Foundation. 1994. (Available from the RSD Information and Publications Group.)

Probation Motor Projects in England and Wales. J P Martin and Douglas Martin. 1994.

Community-based treatment of sex offenders: an evaluation of seven treatment programmes. R Beckett, A Beech, D Fisher and A S Fordham. 1994.

Videotaping children's evidence: an evaluation. Graham Davies, Clare Wilson, Rebecca Mitchell and John Milsom. 1995.

Managing the needs of female prisoners. Allison Morris, Chris Wilkinson, Andrea Tisi, Jane Woodrow and Ann Rockley. 1995.

Local information points for volunteers. Michael Locke, Nick Richards, Lorraine Down, Jon Griffiths and Roger Worgan. 1995.

Mental disorder in remand prisoners. Anthony Maden, Caecilia J. A. Taylor, Deborah Brooke and John Gunn. 1996.

An evaluation of prison work and training. Frances Simon and Claire Corbett. 1996.

The Impact of the National Lottery on the Horse-Race Betting Levy. Simon Field. 1996.

Requests for Publications

Home Office Research Studies from 143 onwards, *Research and Planning Unit Papers, Research Findings and Research Bulletins* can be requested, **subject to availability**, from:

Research and Statistics Directorate
Information and Publications Group
Room 201, Home Office
50 Queen Anne's Gate
London SW1H 9AT
Telephone: 0171-273 2084
Fascimile: 0171-222 0211
Internet: http//www.open.gov.u/home_off/rsdhome.htp
E-mail: rsd.ha apollo @ gtnet.gov.u.

Occasional Papers can be purchased from:
Home Office
Publications Unit
50 Queen Anne's Gate
London SW1H 9AT
Telephone: 0171 273 2302

Home Office Research Studies prior to 143 can be purchased from:

HMSO Publications Centre

(Mail, fax and telephone orders only)
PO Box 276, London SW8 5DT
Telephone orders: 0171-873 9090
General enquiries: 0171-873 0011
(queuing system in operation for both numbers)
Fax orders: 0171-873 8200

*And also from **HMSO Bookshops***